Women and the Chip

Case Studies of the Effects of Informatics on Employment in Canada

by
Heather Menzies

**With editorial and
statistical assistance
by Russell Wilkins**

The Institute for Research on Public Policy
L'Institut de recherches politiques

Montreal

Printed in Canada
ISBN 0 920380 88 3

Legal Deposit First Quarter
Bibliothèque nationale du Québec

The Institute for Research on Public Policy/L'Institut de recherches politiques
2149 Mackay Street
Montreal, Quebec
H3G 2J2

Founded in 1972, THE INSTITUTE FOR RESEARCH ON PUBLIC POLICY is a national organization whose independence and autonomy are ensured by the revenues of an endowment fund, which is supported by the federal and provincial governments and by the private sector. In addition, the Institute receives grants and contracts from governments, corporations, and foundations to carry out specific research projects.

The *raison d'être* of the Institute is threefold:

— To act as a catalyst within the national community by helping to facilitate informed public debate on issues of major public interest

— To stimulate participation by all segments of the national community in the process that leads to public policy making

— To find practical solutions to important public policy problems, thus aiding in the development of sound public policies

The Institute is governed by a Board of Directors, which is the decision-making body, and a Council of Trustees, which advises the board on matters related to the research direction of the Institute. Day-to-day administration of the Institute's policies, programmes, and staff is the responsibility of the president.

The Institute operates in a decentralized way, employing researchers located across Canada. This ensures that research undertaken will include contributions from all regions of the country.

Wherever possible, the Institute will try to promote public understanding of, and discussion on, issues of national importance, whether they be controversial or not. It will publish its research findings with clarity and impartiality. Conclusions or recommendations in the Institute's publications are solely those of the author, and should not be attributed to the Board of Directors, Council of Trustees, or contributors to the Institute.

The president bears final responsibility for the decision to publish a manuscript under the Institute's imprint. In reaching this decision, he is advised on the accuracy and objectivity of a manuscript by both Institute staff and outside reviewers. Publication of a manuscript signifies that it is deemed to be a competent treatment of a subject worthy of public consideration.

Publications of the Institute are published in the language of the author, along with an executive summary in both of Canada's official languages.

iv

Foreword

Technological change based on the miniature computer—the "chip"—is producing a revolution in machines, products, processes, and office organization. The versatile applications the "chip" makes possible are being introduced in a wide range of industrial, commercial, and service operations and in the most diverse employments. Probably no technological revolution has come so quickly or has had a greater impact in so many places—and yet the full extent of the changes and their ultimate consequence are still to be measured and felt. One of the most important—and perhaps the most worrying—will be the impact on jobs and employment.

Most technologically advanced countries have become increasingly concerned about what the micro-electronics revolution will do to people now in employment and to the nature and number of jobs for the future. In November 1979, the Institute produced a report by Zavis Zeman, *The Impacts of Computer/Communications on Employment in Canada: An Overview of Current OECD Debates*. The report concluded that with the present state of knowledge and with so many factors at play, no one really knows what the net employment outcome of the new wave of technological change will be. The report pointed out, however, that there does seem to be an emerging consensus that "overall, it is the women, who form the bulk of information manipulators in Canada, who are expected to bear the brunt of the impact." The Institute has therefore addressed the question of present and foreseeable impacts of office automation on employment of women. The result of this exploration is Heather Menzies' work, *Women and the Chip*.

The study examines four specific cases of the application of micro-electronics to businesses in Canada. It shows how technology eliminated many jobs while transforming others. It brings out the extent to which the impact is likely to be felt in employments to which women in Canada have traditionally turned. It makes clear that these employments will almost certainly not be as plentiful in the future, in relation to the number of women seeking employment, as in the past. It warns that adjustments in education, in training, and in the attitudes both of employers and of women seeking work must occur if serious problems are to be avoided. It brings out both the complexity and the urgency of technological change as a problem and, perhaps, as an opportunity for women who will be looking to employment in the years ahead.

Ms. Menzies' book may lead to discussion on the role of women in employment, on the attitudes of employers toward women, and on the adequacy of our methods of training at a time of rapid change. It may focus new attention on the conclusion of the 1976 report of the Organisation for Economic Co-operation and Development that Canadian education policy needs to be more closely integrated with national policies and economic realities. It could open up a still wider discussion on the social implications of technology.

Gordon Robertson
President
January 1981

Avant-propos

L'évolution de la technologie qu'occasionne le micro-ordinateur—la microplaquette—révolutionne les machines, les produits et les méthodes ainsi que l'organisation des bureaux. La multiplicité des utilisations possibles des microplaquettes est mise à profit dans de nombreuses activités industrielles, commerciales et tertiaires des plus variées. Il s'agit probablement de la révolution technologique la plus rapide et de plus grande portée que nous ayons connue—même s'il reste encore à ressentir et à évaluer toute l'ampleur des changements et de leurs conséquences, dont une des plus importantes (et peut-être des plus inquiétantes) est l'effet sur le travail et l'emploi.

La plupart des pays à forte évolution technologique se préoccupent toujours davantage des répercussions de la révolution microélectronique sur la main-d'oeuvre actuelle, et sur la nature et le type d'emplois futurs. En novembre 1979, l'Institut publiait un rapport de Zavis Zeman intitulé *The Impacts of Computer/Communications on Employment in Canada: An Overview of Current OECD Debates*. Ce rapport concluait que, compte tenu de l'état actuel des connaissances et du nombre de facteurs en jeu, personne ne savait vraiment quel serait le résultat net de cette nouvelle vague de changement technologique en matière d'emploi. Le rapport soulignait néanmoins que l'on semblait s'entendre que, « dans l'ensemble, ce sont les femmes, qui constituent le gros des manipulateurs de l'information au Canada, qui subiront les plus importants contre-coups ». L'Institut s'est donc intéressé aux répercussions actuelles et à venir de l'automatisation du bureau sur l'emploi des femmes. L'étude de Heather Menzies est le résultat de cette exploration.

Le travail examine quatre cas d'utilisation de la microélectronique dans des entreprises canadiennes. Il présente la façon dont la technologie a éliminé nombre d'emplois et en a transformé d'autres. Il indique dans quelle mesure les emplois occupés traditionnellement par les femmes au Canada seront touchés : à l'avenir, ces emplois ne seront certes pas aussi disponibles, compte tenu du nombre de femmes à la recherche d'un emploi. Il nous avertit qu'il faut modifier l'enseignement et la formation ainsi que les attitudes des employeurs et des demandeuses d'emploi si l'on espère éviter de graves problèmes. Il démontre que le changement technologique est à la fois un problème complexe et urgent et, peut-être, une chance qui s'offre aux femmes qui, dans les années à venir, chercheront un emploi.

Le livre de Mme Menzies est à même de susciter des discussions sur le rôle des femmes dans le monde du travail, sur les attitudes des employeurs envers les femmes et sur la pertinence de nos méthodes de formation en cette période d'évolution accélérée. Il pourrait aussi relancer le débat sur la conclusion du rapport de 1976 de l'O.C.D.E. affirmant que la politique d'éducation du Canada doit se conformer davantage aux politiques nationales et aux réalités économiques. Il pourrait enfin susciter une interrogation plus globale sur les implications sociales de la technologie.

Le président,
Gordon Robertson
Janvier 1981

"Canadian women are on a collision course between their continuing concentration in clerical occupations and industry's diminishing requirements in that line of work.''

This report is one of a series of studies examining the probable economic and social impacts of foreseeable technological changes in Canada. The project was done as part of the Institute's Technology and Society Program, directed by Zavis Zeman, and was partially funded by the Labour Market Development Task Force, Employment and Immigration Canada (Contract No. DSS 0 SU80-00191).

Acknowledgements

The existence of this work and the extent to which it enlarges public understanding of office and other forms of information automation are due to the many people who co-operated in its creation. I am especially grateful to those who trusted me with confidential information but who must remain anonymous.

Chief among those who I can name, I wish to thank Zavis Zeman, Director of the Institute's Technology and Society Program, for his guiding vision and enthusiastic support. I also wish to thank Russell Wilkins, whose editorial and statistical contributions were as graciously offered as they were invaluable. Others whose advice and co-operation were indispensible include Al Schackleton (Department of Communications), Keith Newton (Economic Council of Canada), Rosemary Billings (National Action Committee on the Status of Women), Ian Macredie and Henry Pold (Labour Force Survey Division, Statistics Canada), Robert Russel (Orba Ltd.), Hugh McRoberts (Carleton University), Robert McIntosh (Canadian Bankers' Association), Boris Mather (Canadian Federation of Communication Workers), Laraine Singler (Canadian Labour Congress), Bill Reno (United Food and Commercial Workers), Richard Gornitsky (University of Toronto), Stephen Peitchinis (University of Calgary), and my kind and patient husband, Miles Burton.

I am also indebted to the following people for their most useful comments and suggestions at an Institute panel-seminar concerning the orientation of this research: Kelly Butt, Nouella Challenger, Arthur Cordell, L. Hemond, Elizabeth Humphreys, Sheila Isaac, Diane MacKay, Julyan Reid, Gene Schuster, Margaret Smiley, and Ray Vafpa.

The insights are thanks to the people who contributed to this study. The errors are mine.

Heather Menzies
Ottawa
December 1980

The Author

Heather Menzies is a freelance writer living in Ottawa. A social science graduate of McGill University, she has worked as a journalist for the *Edmonton Journal, Report on Farming*, and the *Winnipeg Tribune*. She has freelanced for the *Financial Post Magazine, Macleans, and Weekend Magazine*, as well as for CFRN T.V. in Edmonton and CBC in Winnipeg. She has worked as a documentary film maker in Montreal, and more recently as a policy researcher-writer in Ottawa. Her book, *The Railroad's Not Enough: Canada Now*, was published by Clarke, Irwin in 1978.

Table of Contents

List of Figures

List of Tables

Executive Summary

This report, in nine chapters, looks at the effects the new technology of informatics will have on women employed in the service-producing sector. Informatics has evolved out of two electronic technologies: computers and telecommunications. It involves the automation of all phases of information manipulation from gathering to dissemination.

Chapter One traces the history of women's presence in the labour force. Between 1953 and 1979, the participation rate of women doubled to over 48 per cent. The proportion of working married women has increased dramatically to over 44 per cent. Some projections show these trends continuing, to the point where up to two thirds of all Canadian women may be participating in the labour force by the year 2000. Most of the employment growth over the last twenty years has been concentrated in the service sector. In 1980, the tertiary sector accounted for 80 per cent of all women in the paid labour force. The continued concentration of women's employment in clerical occupations could pose a serious problem if informatics has a negative impact on clerical-type, information-handling jobs.

Chapter Two introduces the "office of the future." The push for increased productivity in the office has accelerated the introduction of computers to reduce clerical work. This has involved the automation of information-handling work functions, not only in offices, but wherever information handling occurs. The decreasing size and price of microprocessors has further speeded their introduction. The four case studies in Chapters Three to Six look at the impact of informatics on employment, especially of women in clerical positions.

There appears to be a polarization of approach to informatics innovation. The *télématique* approach envisages one central electronic utility, accessible anywhere, that integrates the multi-functional, decision-making support system of the company. The *privatique* approach would produce a diffusion of many, independent informatics loci, with little need for a central computer. The traditional office would remain, although the support equipment and job functions would be transformed.

Several factors outside the technology itself will spur or retard its implementation. Increased productivity, business competition, and government support would accelerate the diffusion process, while energy costs, lack of a government policy on telecommunications, or union resistance would hinder its development.

Chapter Three is a case study of a large, diversified Canadian corporation engaged in transportation and communications. The data-processing department was increasing the capacity of the original computer system at the same time that the administrative services department was introducing word-processing machines and other office automation equipment. An interdepartmental study group drafted a master plan calling for a telecommunications grid connecting senior and local corporate desks. The grid included computing, facsimile document transmission, and electronic message sending. The objective was twofold: increased effectiveness of decision-making staff and decreased costs.

Office automation profoundly altered employment patterns. There was a sharp reduction in clerical job openings accompanied by a major demand for professional and managerial people. Significantly, only 2 of 130 displaced clerical workers advanced to the professional ranks. Informatics disproportionately reduced the labour content of low-skilled jobs, while increasing the skill content of professional information work. With entry-level job requirements rising faster than work-force skills, there is a fear that would-be clerical workers might become potentially unemployable. The case study also points out changes in the type of secretarial skills required. A different set of non-traditional, technical skills is now needed.

Chapter Four is a case study of an insurance company where information work accounts for 90 per cent of employment. Insurance has been a major source of jobs, particularly for women, in the last twenty years. However, growth has slowed in the last five years, and for women, employment actually decreased. In the first phase of informatics, a computer was acquired for data processing. In the second phase, electronically based information became accessible to professionals throughout the company, and departments were realigned according to task content. In the third phase, specific work functions were automated, such as issuing of promotional material, processing premiums, and monitoring birthdays.

Automation seriously changed the demand for particular occupations and the skills needed. There was a reduction in the number of clerical operations and in the labour content of the insurance work. There was a reduction in the need for supervisors, accompanied by a transfer of previously professional functions onto clerical staff. Such changes allowed ''jobless growth'' and expansion into new business without new staff. A concentration of growth at the professional level meant fewer new job openings for clerical people. The widening skills gap between clerical and other work shut clerical workers off from upward mobility. Clerical workers in insurance now face unemployment because they do not have the necessary skills.

Chapter Five is a case study of the banking industry. As in the previous two case studies, there was a rationalization and amalgamation of jobs and an upgrading of skill requirements for job recruits. With automation, the banks have introduced new services and are considering automated teller machines. The expansion of banking services created new jobs with a much lower clerical component. In the future, entry-level bank work may require a university degree. Banks are no longer a haven for clerical-level work. The net employment effects of automation are obscured by a blurring of job distinctions between clerical and professional categories as well as by an increasing use of part-time workers. As far as strictly office automation is concerned, banks have differed in whether they use the *télématique* or the *privatique* approach.

Chapter Six is a case study of the effects of electronic cash registers and optical scanners in supermarkets. Even in preliminary phases, rationalization of store administration, increased productivity, and reduced hours of labour have resulted. There is a failure to replace workers such as cashiers, and jobless growth rather than lay-offs.

The four case studies looked at employment in industries where women are heavily concentrated. Informatics created new work, but largely in professional and managerial ranks where women are a minority. Informatics seemed to be eroding the need for traditional clerical work.

Chapter Seven summarizes the case study observations. Perhaps the most significant is that the productivity of clerical workers was increasing. This was achieved by a reduction in the labour content of clerical functions and by an amalgamation of formerly distinct jobs. Fewer clerical operations were needed for each type of service provided, with an accompanying reduction in supervisory requirements. In the case studies, it seemed that productivity gains were faster where a *télématique* approach was used. The corporations tended to view office automation as part of a larger transformation of their entire information-related work functions.

Employment-related concerns identified by the study fall into three categories. First, informatics generated extra employment, but only in specialist ranks. There was a growing mismatch between the training and skills of female job seekers and the types of employment being created. The forms of clerical unemployment were subtle: there were fewer job openings and more unfilled job vacancies. As clerical employment declined, part-time work became important. Second, as clerical labour demand decreased, virtually none of the clerical workers was transferred to the expanding professional ranks. This was partly due to attitudes of management and partly due to a lack of technical knowledge on the part of employees. Structural barriers to upward mobility included the skills gap, a concentration in one area, and management indifference to part-time workers. The third concern was the lower quality of working life. Automation tended to emphasize quantity of output rather than the skills or experience of the operator.

Chapter Eight presents four scenarios of probable outcomes from informatics diffusion. There are two critical variables. Productivity assumes a ''high'' gain value of 50 per cent and a ''low'' gain value of 33 per cent. Diffusion assumes a ''slow'' period of twenty years and a ''fast'' period of fifteen years. The scenarios project a mismatch between skills and jobs that could result in alarmingly high rates of unemployment among female clerical workers. The solutions suggested by the scenarios are to steer young women away from seeking clerical-skill-level work, to help women already in the clerical ghettos to move out, and to narrow the skills gap.

In the conclusions are recommendations on how to reduce the lack of mobility and potential structural unemployment of clerical workers in the 1990s. The author suggests several broad initiatives for government: a public education campaign to alert women about the poor prospects for clerical jobs and to encourage job mobility; retailoring of existing manpower training courses; and a special task force of government, industry, and labour to look at the implications of the diffusion of informatics on employment in general.

More specifically, governments should launch programmes to increase the computer literacy of Canadians. Government manpower training for women should orient them toward more promising areas of industrial activity and employment. Apprenticeship programmes should combine technical education and skills training.

Counselling programmes should be funded to help equip women for occupational mobility and to establish self-help endeavours. Since so many clerical and information staff work part-time, governments should move to provide them with benefits comparable to full-time workers. More research is needed on the effects of informatics on small business and on employment and jobs in general.

Canadian women are vulnerable because their jobs are concentrated in areas being swept away by information technology. They are threatened because they lack the financial and educational mobility to adapt. If they are not helped to adapt, their unemployment could have serious consequences both for them and for the national economy. If they can adapt, they could help to boost Canada into a buoyant post-industrial condition. The determination of which result is to ensue will depend on early and effective action by governments, employers, and women themselves.

Abrégé

Les neuf chapitres de ce rapport portent sur les effets éventuels de l'informatique sur les femmes employées dans le secteur des services. Cette nouvelle technologie tire son origine de deux technologies électroniques, soit les ordinateurs et les télécommunications. Elle implique l'automatisation de toutes les étapes de la manipulation de l'information, de la collecte à la diffusion.

Le premier chapitre trace l'historique de la présence des femmes dans la population active. De 1953 à 1979, cette présence a doublé : plus de 48 % des femmes travaillent aujourd'hui. La proportion de femmes mariées a connu une augmentation dramatique : plus de 44 % d'entre elles travaillent. Selon certaines projections, il se pourrait que près des deux tiers des femmes travaillent en l'an 2000. Au cours des vingt dernières années, la croissance de l'emploi s'est surtout faite dans les services. En 1980, 80 % des femmes salariées travaillaient dans le secteur tertiaire. Cette concentration permanente des femmes dans le travail de bureau pourrait avoir de sérieuses conséquences si l'informatique exerce des effets négatifs sur le travail de bureau relié au traitement de l'information.

Le chapitre deux présente le « bureau de l'avenir ». La recherche d'un accroissement de la productivité dans les bureaux a favorisé l'introduction accélérée d'ordinateurs destinés à réduire le travail de bureau. Cela a entraîné l'automatisation du traitement de l'information, non seulement dans les bureaux, mais partout où cette activité a lieu. Ce phénomène s'est produit d'autant plus rapidement que la taille et le prix des microprocesseurs diminuaient. Les quatre études individuelles qui constituent les chapitres trois à six illustrent les répercussions de l'informatique sur l'emploi, et en particulier sur celui des femmes dans les bureaux.

Les approches de l'innovation en informatique semblent se polariser. L'approche *télématique* prévoit un central électronique, accessible de partout et intégrant toutes les fonctions de prise de décisions de la compagnie. L'approche *privatique* favorise une multiplicité de centres informatiques, sans grand besoin d'un recours à un ordinateur central. On conserverait le bureau traditionnel tout en transformant les fonctions et le matériel de soutien.

Certains facteurs, étrangers à la technologie comme telle, favoriseront ou retarderont sa mise en oeuvre. Un accroissement de la productivité, la concurrence et l'appui du gouvernement pourraient la favoriser, tandis que les coûts de l'énergie, l'absence d'une politique des télécommunications ou la résistance des syndicats pourraient la retarder.

Le chapitre trois renferme une étude individuelle d'une grande société canadienne diversifiée engagée dans les transports et les communications. Le service de traitement de l'information était à accroître la capacité du système d'ordinateurs original, alors que les services administratifs introduisaient des machines de traitement des mots et d'autre matériel de bureau automatique. Un groupe d'études interservices présenta un projet de plan directeur qui proposait une grille des télécommunications reliant les bureaux de la direction et les bureaux locaux. La grille prévoyait les installations de calcul, la transmission par facsimilé et l'envoi électronique de messages. L'objectif était double : l'accroissement de l'efficacité du personnel de décision et la diminution des coûts.

L'automatisation du bureau modifia profondément les tendances d'emploi. Les offres d'emploi de bureau diminuèrent sensiblement, alors qu'augmentait de beaucoup la demande de professionnels et de gestionnaires. Fait à noter, seulement deux des cent trente employés de bureau évincés accédèrent aux rangs professionnels. L'informatique a réduit de façon disproportionnée la dimension travail des emplois à faible spécialisation par rapport à l'augmentation de la dimension spécialisation du travail professionnel relatif à l'information. Comme les exigences d'emploi augmentent plus rapidement que la spécialisation de la main-d'oeuvre, on craint que ceux qui aspirent au travail de bureau ne trouvent éventuellement plus de travail. L'étude de cas fait aussi état des changements prévus dans les exigences relatives aux compétences dans le travail de secrétariat. On a maintenant besoin de nouvelles compétences techniques non traditionnelles.

Le chapitre quatre renferme une étude individuelle d'une société d'assurances où le traitement de l'information représente 90 % de l'emploi. Au cours des vingt dernières années, les assurances ont constitué une importante source d'emplois, surtout pour les femmes. La croissance a toutefois ralenti ces cinq dernières années, et l'emploi des femmes a même diminué. Dans la première phase de l'informatique, on s'est procuré un ordinateur pour le traitement des données. Dans la seconde phase, les professionnels de la société ont pu avoir accès à de l'information électronique, et les services ont été réorganisés en fonction des tâches. Dans la troisième phase, on a automatisé diverses fonctions, telles que l'envoi de publicité, le traitement des primes et la surveillance des anniversaires.

L'automatisation a entraîné une modification profonde de la demande, dans certaines professions, et de certaines compétences. On a constaté une diminution des tâches de bureau et de la dimension travail du travail d'assurances. Il y a eu une diminution du besoin de surveillants, qui s'est accompagnée d'un transfert de tâches, auparavant professionnelles, au personnel de bureau. De tels changements permirent une « croissance sans emploi » et une expansion sans augmentation de personnel. La concentration de la croissance dans la catégorie professionnelle s'est traduite par une baisse des offres d'emploi pour le personnel de bureau. L'écart croissant des compétences entre le travail de bureau et les autres types de travail a privé les employés de bureau de toute mobilité ascendante. Les travailleurs de bureau du domaine des assurances font face au chômage par manque des compétences nécessaires.

Le chapitre cinq renferme une étude individuelle de l'industrie des banques. Ici comme ailleurs, on a assisté à une rationalisation et à un regroupement des emplois ainsi qu'à un accroissement des exigences pour les nouveaux employés. L'automatisation a permis l'introduction de nouveaux services; on envisage aujourd'hui le recours aux caissiers automatiques. L'expansion des services banquaires a créé de nouveaux emplois qui exigent moins de travail de bureau. Il faudra peut-être à l'avenir être diplômé d'université pour être embauché par une banque. Les banques ne sont plus le refuge des travailleurs de bureau. L'affaiblissement de la distinction entre le travail de bureau et les emplois professionnels, et le recours accru aux employés à temps partiel obscurcit la nature précise des effets de l'automatisation. En ce qui a trait à l'automatisation des bureaux comme telle, certaines banques adoptent l'approche *télématique*, les autres, l'approche *privatique*.

Le chapitre six renferme une étude des effets des caisses enregistreuses électroniques et des lecteurs optiques dans les supermarchés. Même dans les phases préliminaires, on a remarqué une rationalisation de l'administration des magasins, une productivité accrue et une diminution des heures de travail. On ne remplace pas des travailleurs comme les caissières et on favorise une croissance sans création d'emplois plutôt que des licenciements.

Les quatre études de cas ont porté sur l'emploi dans des industries où il existe une forte concentration de femmes. L'informatique crée de nouveaux emplois, mais surtout dans les secteurs professionnels et administratifs où les femmes sont en minorité. L'informatique semble saper le besoin traditionnel de travailleurs de bureau.

Le chapitre sept résume les observations des études individuelles, la plus importante étant peut-être relative à l'augmentation de la productivité des travailleurs de bureau en raison de la réduction de la dimension travail des tâches de bureau et du regroupement de certains emplois. Chaque service fourni exigeait moins d'activités et aussi moins de surveillance. Il semble, du moins dans les cas étudiés, que les gains de productivité soient plus rapides avec l'approche *télématique*. Les sociétés avaient tendance à considérer l'automatisation du bureau comme une facette d'une transformation globale de l'ensemble des activités relatives à l'information.

Les questions relatives à l'emploi identifiées dans le cadre de l'étude se rangent dans trois catégories. En premier lieu, l'informatique a créé de nouveaux emplois mais seulement dans la catégorie des spécialistes. On remarquait un écart croissant entre la formation et la compétence des demandeuses d'emploi et le genre d'emplois créés. Le chômage relatif au travail de bureau avait un caractère subtil : il y avait moins d'offres d'emploi et on ne comblait pas les postes vacants. Le déclin du travail de bureau s'accompagnait d'une augmentation du travail à temps partiel. En deuxième lieu, suite à la baisse de la demande de travailleurs de bureau, à peu près aucun n'a pu accéder aux rangs professionnels en pleine croissance. Cet état de fait dépendait en partie des attitudes de la direction et en partie du manque de connaissances techniques chez les employés. L'écart des compétences, leur concentration dans un domaine et l'indifférence de la direction face aux travailleurs à temps partiel représentent autant de barrières à la mobilité ascendante. Une baisse du niveau de la qualité du milieu de travail constituait la troisième préoccupation. L'automatisation tendait à faire porter l'accent sur le rendement plutôt que sur les aptitudes ou l'expérience de l'opérateur.

Le chapitre huit présente quatre scénarios des conséquences probables de la diffusion de l'informatique. Il existe deux variables critiques. La productivité suppose une limite supérieure des gains de 50 % et une limite inférieure de 33 %, tandis que la diffusion suppose une période « lente » de vingt ans et une période « rapide » de quinze ans. Les scénarios prévoient un écart entre les compétences et les emplois qui pourrait provoquer un chômage dangereusement élevé chez les travailleuses de bureau. Ils proposent comme solutions d'inciter les jeunes femmes à délaisser la recherche d'emplois dans les bureaux, d'aider celles qui s'y trouvent déjà à quitter ces ghettos et de réduire l'écart des compétences.

Les conclusions présentent des recommandations sur la façon de réduire le manque de mobilité et le chômage structurel éventuel des travailleurs de bureau au cours des années 1990. L'auteur trace les grandes lignes des initiatives à être prises par l'État : un programme d'éducation publique destiné à avertir les femmes des mauvaises perspectives dans le domaine du travail de bureau et à encourager la mobilité professionnelle; une refonte des cours de formation professionnelle; et un groupe d'étude spécial, regroupant des représentants du gouvernement, de l'entreprise et des syndicats, chargé d'étudier les implications de la diffusion de l'informatique sur l'emploi en général.

Plus précisément, les gouvernements devraient mettre en oeuvre des programmes destinés à accroître la connaissance des ordinateurs chez les Canadiens. La formation professionnelle offerte aux femmes par l'État devrait les orienter vers des secteurs d'activité industrielle et d'emploi plus prometteurs. Les programmes d'apprentissage devraient allier instruction technique et formation des compétences.

On devrait financer des programmes d'orientation destinés à préparer les femmes à la mobilité professionnelle et à mettre sur pied des activités d'autoformation. Compte tenu de l'importante proportion du personnel de bureau et d'information travaillant à temps partiel, les gouvernements devraient prendre des mesures afin de leur procurer des avantages comparables à ceux dont jouissent les travailleurs à temps plein. Il faut effectuer davantage de recherches sur les effets de l'informatique sur les petites entreprises ainsi que sur l'emploi et le travail en général.

Les femmes canadiennes sont vulnérables car leurs emplois se concentrent dans des domaines qu'envahit la technologie de l'information. Elles sont menacées car elles ne disposent pas de la mobilité financière ou éducative qui leur permettrait de s'adapter. Si on ne les aide pas à le faire, leur chômage risque d'avoir, à la fois pour elles et pour l'économie du pays, de graves conséquences. Si elles réussissent à s'adapter, elles pourraient aider le Canada à s'ancrer dans une position post-industrielle ferme. Une action rapide et efficace de la part des gouvernements, des employeurs et des femmes elles-mêmes déterminera de quel côté penchera la balance.

Introduction

Informatics: Hopes and Fears

Canada is entering the post-industrial age borne on an electronic chariot called *informatics*, the nature of which few people understand, the impact of which few Canadians will escape.

The child of two separate but increasingly interwoven electronic technologies—computers and telecommunications—informatics will complete the process begun when the raw material of information, data, was first transformed into an electronic idiom back in the 1950s, and the new industry known as data processing came into being.

Informatics involves the automation of all phases of information manipulation—such as its gathering, integrating, storing, and disseminating. It is a process that depends on the complementary transformation of information from passive paper to dynamic electronic storage and retrieval, and that may eventually lead to the emergence of a microelectronics-based, post-industrial "information economy." Such changes are likely to affect employment wherever information forms a major component of the work function.

While futurists already speak of what they call the "information sector," economists have yet to specify a meaningful definition of the "output" from information work in, say, the resource-extracting or manufacturing industries. Studies have found, though, that information handling constitutes roughly 10 per cent of employment in primary industries, a third in secondary industries, and nearly half of all service-sector work (Serafini *et al.*, 1978, p. 87). So the effect should be concentrated in the service sector, whose rapid growth over the last thirty years has been credited with forestalling what might have been massive unemployment as a result of the first wave of automation, which spread through industry (factories, processing plants, and so on) in the 1950s, 1960s, and 1970s.

Within the service sector, women are particularly affected, since they are concentrated in occupations where information manipulation and related clerical-type operations constitute much of their work. These occupations include secretaries, filing and other office clerks, bank tellers, cashiers, key-punch operators, telephone operators, mail handlers, and related supervisory personnel. Women account for over 90 per cent of employment

1

in most of those occupations. In all of them, the work involves physically or mechanically manipulating information in some basic way—transcribing, typing, filing, collating, copying, or posting it.

Some analysts (cited by Valaskakis, 1979, p. 57) label this work "non-productive," since it supposedly does not add to the information's value. However, while such work does not significantly change the content of the information (such as by analysing or interpreting it), it does add to the usefulness of the information, if only by making it more readily accessible. Nevertheless, it is the clerical jobs that are said to be under threat from informatics, while professional and technical information work is considered to be the most promising area for future employment growth.

Hypotheses about the "post-industrial" economy (Bell, 1973, pp. 112-19) assume that once information is in an electronic idiom, it will become the energizing agent that non-renewable resources have been to the industrial economy. In other words, instead of information playing a peripheral role (as back-up and feedback), it will become the central focus or axis around which the post-industrial society will take shape.

Informatics companies, including both equipment and software systems vendors, will replace the oil companies and auto manufacturers as the major growth industries of our economy. Running them will require a new breed of information professionals specializing in information flows, as well as in the packaging and marketing of intellectual products.

Overall, the work-force will apply a more sophisticated range of skills and knowledge—both technical and general—and will be freer than ever before to work alone or in groups, at home or in large offices.

It promises to be an exciting age, one in which Marshall McLuhan's "global village" (McLuhan and Fiore, 1967) becomes a universe of "wired heads" (Rockman, 1980), with the wisdom of the world's best libraries and the trivia of its classified ads instantly accessible to anyone with the money to pay for this information or fortunate enough to live where government policy makes it freely available as a public service.

The transition period, though, could be extremely painful. Less competitive industries and industrial practices, including old-fashioned information-handling systems, will be squeezed out of existence. Thus, unless the work-force affected, such as female clerical workers, rapidly develops alternative skills, knowledge, and the informatics aptitude to meet the employment demands of post-industrial work, Canada could experience severe structural unemployment.

According to a report by the Organisation for Economic Co-operation and Development (Seear, 1971, p. 15) on women's re-entry into the labour market,

> The introduction of the computer has slowed up the rate of increase in the demand for clerical workers but has not led to an absolute reduction. In the long run, however,

when the full effects of office automation have become apparent it is reasonable to expect a reduction in the demand for clerical workers.

A literature overview of anticipated informatics impacts prepared by The Institute for Research on Public Policy (Zeman, 1979, p. 44) concluded that "Overall, it is the women, who form the bulk of the information manipulators in the service sector, who are expected to bear the brunt of the impact."

As this report will demonstrate, the future seems already to have begun.

The first two chapters will serve as an introduction to the technology of informatics and will identify the people whose information work the new technology is affecting. Chapter One will trace the history of women's participation in the work-force, including their growing concentration in and share of the (up to now) expanding clerical occupations. It will also examine predictions concerning the female labour force to the year 2000, in terms of participation rates as well as occupational orientations.

Chapter Two will probe the mysteries of informatics and telematics. Each of these terms implies the integration of computer and telecommunication technologies, and the automation of information systems this integration makes possible. The term telematics, however, is also equated with a certain form of integration—more of a merger into one universal electronic utility. This approach will be discussed and contrasted with other approaches.

Chapter Three will focus on the specific forms of informatics associated with office automation, and will feature a case study illustrating how one "office of the future" requires a very different type of work-force.

Chapters Four, Five, and Six will describe the forms and effects of informatics in insurance, banking, and retail trade, adopting different perspectives for greater insight.

A closely focused view, based on company case studies, is essential to pin down the often subtle and indirect effects of the technology. As the studies themselves demonstrate, the results can vary substantially from one industry to the next and according to the approach of management and the motivation of workers. Unfortunately, the inescapable narrowness of case studies of individual companies restricts the relevance of such findings. To compensate for this somewhat, Chapters Five and Six will provide a larger frame of reference based on industry-wide studies.

After Chapter Seven synthesizes the previous chapters, Chapter Eight will expand the frame of reference still further, by testing some of the key research findings in a number of transition scenarios. Using as a target population the projected number of women seeking clerical work in successive five-year intervals up to the year 2000, and testing two possible rates of productivity gain and technology diffusion, the scenarios will predict the extent of structural unemployment possible during Canada's transition into the post-industrial age.

The final chapter will set out recommendations on how the transition can be made easier by preventing the undesirable scenarios from happening.

Chapter One

Women in the Labour Force: Where They Are and What They Are Doing

Women's increasing presence and permanence in the labour market is one of the most significant developments in Canadian society over the last thirty years. That pattern is expected to continue as social conditions lead to an increase in the number of single parents, as harsh economic realities necessitate the participation of both spouses in the work-force, and as changing life-styles make paid employment almost as permanent a fixture in women's lives as it is for men.

In 1953, the labour-force participation rate of women was 23 per cent; by 1979, it had more than doubled, to 49 per cent. During the 1970s alone, the number of women in the labour force rose by 62 per cent. In May 1980, 4.6 million Canadian women were either working or looking for work.[1]

Perhaps the most important factor in this growth has been the increasing similarity of participation rates between single and married women. According to labour-force data from Canadian censuses,[2] in 1951, less than 10 per cent of married women worked outside the home (or were looking for such work), compared to 56 per cent of single women. By 1976, the percentage of working married women had risen to 44 per cent, while the percentage of working single women was stable at 57 per cent. In other words, over the course of that twenty-five-year period, the gap in participation rates between single and married women had shrunk from 46 to 13 points. This gap is expected to diminish still further through the 1980s.

Figure 1.1 and Table 1.1 summarize a number of projections for women's labour-force participation to the year 2001. Projected rates for the end of the century vary from lows in the general range of present-day female participation rates, to highs not very different from those currently observed in Sweden. All of the studies project increasing female participation in the labour force at least until the end of the 1980s.

The figures shown from the early Goracz, Lithwick, and Stone (1971) study done for the Central Mortgage and Housing Corporation illustrate the bias toward underestimation bequeathed from past projections. Likewise, the Denton, Feaver, and Spencer (1979) study done for the Economic Council of Canada cannot be discounted just because its high projection for 1981 had already been reached by 1979 and its medium projection, exceeded by two

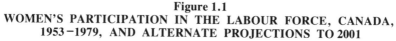

Figure 1.1
**WOMEN'S PARTICIPATION IN THE LABOUR FORCE, CANADA,
1953−1979, AND ALTERNATE PROJECTIONS TO 2001**

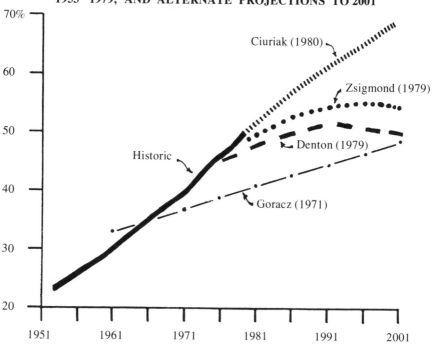

points. However, this discrepancy does justify suspicions that the Denton *et al.* projections for later years may very well be on the low side also.

The intermediate values projected by Zsigmond (1979) for The Institute for Research on Public Policy show female participation increasing fairly rapidly until about 1990, and then continuing to increase, but much more slowly, until 2001.

Ciuriak and Sims' (1980) projections for the Department of Finance more closely coincide with the existing pattern in Scandinavia and emerging trends and projections in the United States. They suggest a 40 per cent increase in the female labour force by 1990—an additional 1.8 million women—compared to an increase of 25 per cent—1.1 million women—projected by the Denton *et al.* study.

Such an increase could compensate for the feared labour shortage resulting from a diminishing number of entry-age workers as the Big Generation (from the post-war baby boom) (Kettle, 1980) moves beyond the school-leaving age bracket. But this projected increase could also strain the job market's absorption capacity. Not only are women already concentrated in a few occupations, largely within the service sector, but those occupations and the service sector generally are becoming somewhat less than the horn of employment plenty that they once were.

Table 1.1
WOMEN'S PARTICIPATION IN THE LABOUR FORCE, CANADA,
1953−1979, AND ALTERNATE PROJECTIONS TO 2001
(percentage of women aged 15 and over)

Year	Historic[a]	Ciuriak[b] (1980)	Zsigmond[c] (1979)	Denton[d] (1979)	Goracz[e] (1971)
1953	23.2	23.2			
1960	28.5	28.5			
1961					32.6
1965	33.3	33.3			
1966	35.4				
1970	38.4	38.4			
1971	39.4				32.9
1975		43.9			
1976	45.2			45.0	
1978	47.8		47.8		
1979	48.9	48.6			
1980					
1981			48.9	47.8	41.0
1985		55.6			
1986			52.8	49.9	
1990		60.8			
1991			54.6	51.6	44.3
1995		64.3			
1996			55.1	50.6	
2000		68.0	54.6		
2001				49.9	48.7

Note: a. Based on Labour Force Surveys: old series from 1953−1965, new series from 1966−1979.
    b. Average of high and low projections (which are shown as 70.6% and 65.3%, respectively, by the year 2000).
    c. Only one series of projections given.
    d. Based on medium fertility, immigration and mortality assumptions. Average of high and low projections (which are shown as 54.1% and 45.7%, respectively, by the year 2001).
    e. Based on census data; only one series of projections given.
Source: Prepared from data given in Statistics Canada (1980*d*; 1979*a*), Ciuriak and Sims (1980), Zsigmond (1979), Denton *et al.* (1979), and Goracz *et al.* (1971).

As Figure 1.2 and Table 1.2 demonstrate, most of the employment growth over the last twenty years has been concentrated in the service-producing, tertiary sector of the economy. During the 1970s alone, 85 per cent of the new jobs created (two million) were in this sector, which increased its share of employment from 30 to 60 per cent of working Canadians. Not surprisingly, with the tertiary sector's boom corresponding to the period in which women's labour-force participation was rapidly escalating, women have become more concentrated in this than in any other sector. In May 1980, the service-producing *industries* accounted for 81 per cent of all women in the paid labour force.

Turning now from industrial to occupational classifications of employment, Figure 1.3 and Table 1.3 demonstrate the persistence and degree of

Figure 1.2
EMPLOYMENT BY MAJOR INDUSTRIAL SECTOR, CANADA, 1951−1978
(percentage of total employed)

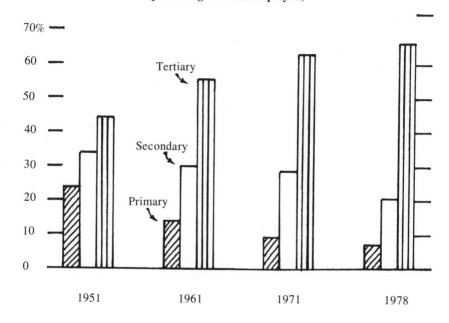

Table 1.2
EMPLOYMENT BY MAJOR INDUSTRIAL SECTOR, CANADA, 1951−1978
(percentage of all employed)

Year	Primary[a]	Secondary[b]	Tertiary[c]	Total	N (x1000)
1951	22.8	33.3	43.9	100.0	5,097
1961	14.2	30.2	55.5	100.0	6,005
1971	9.1	28.2	62.6	100.0	8,078
1975	7.5	26.7	65.7	100.0	9,284
1978	7.3	25.9	66.8	100.0	9,972

Note: a. Agriculture, forestry, fishing and trapping, mining.
    b. Manufacturing and construction.
    c. Transportation and communications, trade, finance, insurance and real estate, community,
        business and personal services, public administration.
Source: Statistics Canada (1980*d*), Table 5.12.

female occupational segregation over the last fifty years. It also highlights the fact that clerical work has replaced domestic service as the pillar of female employment in Canada. It is interesting to note that most women in the ''professional and technical'' category are teachers or nurses.

In 1979, clerical, sales, or service *occupations* accounted for two thirds of all Canadian women in the paid labour force—roughly the same proportion as in 1971. Clerical workers alone accounted for roughly a third of all working women—again basically unchanged from 1971 (Dept. of Labour, Women's Bureau, 1980*a*, 1980*b*). It is worth noting, however, that women maintained this clerical concentration partially at the expense of men. Female clerical employment grew by 12 per cent between 1975 and 1979, while total clerical employment increased only 9 per cent, because the number of male clerical workers declined by 0.5 per cent (Statistics Canada, 1980*a*).

Figure 1.4 and Table 1.4 show what has been happening to female clerical employment growth: it seems to be levelling off. For the first time in twenty years, the growth in female clerical employment over the period between 1975 and 1979 (12 per cent) fell far short of the increase in the

Figure 1.3
PROFILE OF MALE AND FEMALE LABOUR FORCE,
BY OCCUPATIONAL GROUPING, CANADA, 1931−1971
(percentage of experienced labour force, based onc ensus data)

FEMALES

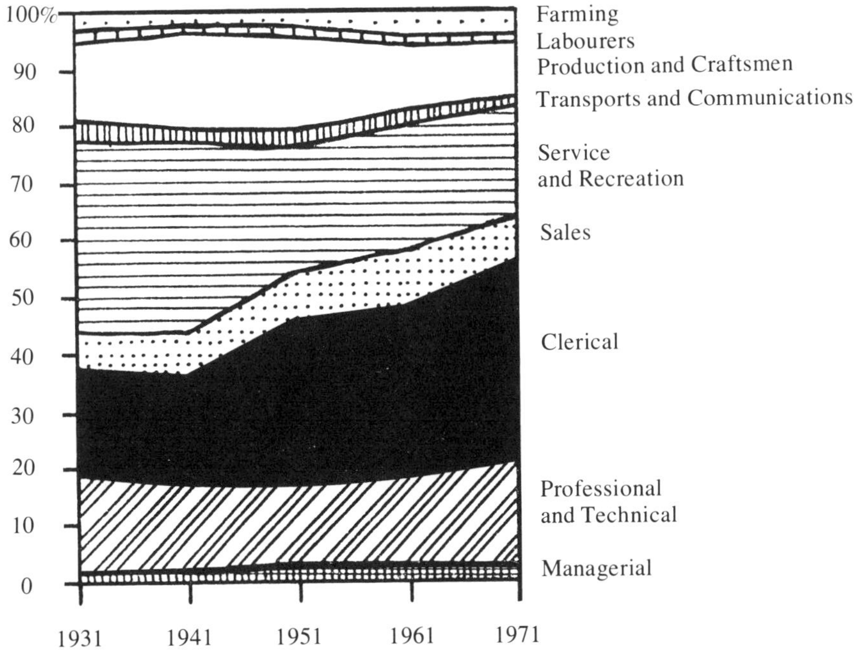

Source: Prepared from data given in Statistics Canada (1978*c*), Table 1.

Figure 1.3 (continued)

MALES

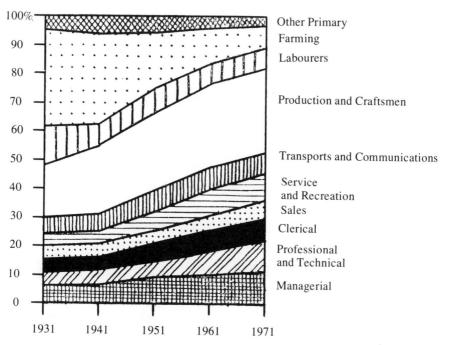

female labour force (20 per cent). This continued concentration of women's employment in clerical occupations poses a potentially serious problem, particularly in light of the projected growth in the female labour force and the minimal shift in women's job orientations from traditionally female occupations.

Women have increased their employment and share of employment in the expanding managerial and professional occupations. Between 1975 and 1980, the number of women in these occupations increased by 24 per cent to nearly one million. Similarly, women's enrolment in non-traditional university programmes has been increasing substantially. In 1977, for instance, women represented 30 per cent of commerce students, compared to 7 per cent in 1962 (Dale, 1980, p. 17). Between 1975 and 1979, the number of female university graduates in the labour force increased 44 per cent. However, university graduates still represented less than 10 per cent of the female labour force in 1979 (Statistics Canada, 1980*c*, 1979*b*).

An attitude survey of female high-school students in the Toronto area (Jackson and Williams, 1974) found, among girls from well-to-do families, a marked shift in job orientation away from traditional female occupational categories and toward employment in the hard sciences; in addition, the

Table 1.3
OCCUPATIONS, BY SEX, CANADA, 1931–1971
(percentage of experienced labour force)

Sex Year	Mana-gerial	Prof./Tech.	Cler-ical	Sales	Service/Recreat.	Transp./Comm.	Product./Crafts.	Labourers	Farming	Fishing/Hunting	Logging	Mining	Total[a]	N (x 1000)[b]
Males														
1931	6.5	3.9	4.7	5.0	4.2	5.8	18.6	13.4	33.7	1.4	1.3	1.7	100.0	3,245
1941	6.6	4.7	4.8	4.4	4.5	6.0	23.8	7.6	31.6	1.5	2.4	2.1	100.0	3,352
1951	9.4	5.4	6.3	4.6	6.6	7.3	27.4	8.1	19.5	1.3	2.5	1.6	100.0	4,114
1961	10.5	7.8	7.1	5.8	8.7	7.7	28.9	7.1	12.5	0.7	1.7	1.4	100.0	4,694
1971	11.4	11.6	7.1	6.1	9.3	7.5	29.5	7.2	7.7	0.5	1.0	1.2	100.0	5,649
Females														
1931	1.6	17.8	18.0	7.0	33.8	2.4	14.0	1.7	3.6	0.1	-	-	100.0	663
1941	2.0	15.7	18.6	7.1	34.2	1.7	17.0	1.4	2.3	0.0	-	-	100.0	831
1951	3.3	14.5	28.1	8.7	21.4	2.9	16.5	1.8	2.8	0.0	-	-	100.0	1,162
1961	3.3	15.8	29.6	8.6	23.0	2.2	11.9	1.2	4.4	0.0	0.0	-	100.0	1,764
1971	3.3	18.2	34.5	7.9	19.7	1.5	9.7	1.3	3.8	-	-	-	100.0	2,960
Total														
1931	5.7	6.2	7.0	5.3	9.2	5.1	17.8	11.4	28.6	1.2	1.1	1.4	100.0	3,908
1941	5.7	6.9	7.5	5.0	10.4	5.1	22.4	6.4	25.8	1.2	1.9	1.7	100.0	4,183
1951	8.1	7.4	11.1	5.5	9.9	6.3	25.0	6.7	15.8	1.0	1.9	1.2	100.0	5,276
1961	8.6	10.0	13.2	6.5	12.6	6.2	24.3	5.5	10.3	0.5	1.3	1.0	100.0	6,458
1971	8.6	13.8	16.2	6.7	12.8	5.5	22.9	5.2	6.4	0.3	0.7	0.8	100.0	8,639

Notes: a. Excluding those members of the experienced labour force for whom no occupation was specified. Totals may not add to 100 due to rounding. A hypen (-) indicates that there were less than 100 persons in the category.
b. Including those for whom no occupation was stated.
Source: Calculated from data given in Statistics Canada (1978c), Table 1.

Figure 1.4
GROWTH OF FEMALE LABOUR FORCE AND FEMALE CLERICAL EMPLOYMENT, CANADA, 1961−1979

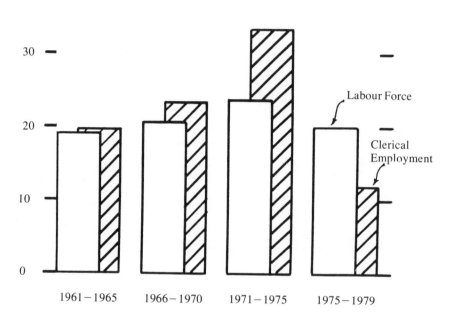

Table 1.4
GROWTH OF FEMALE LABOUR FORCE AND FEMALE CLERICAL EMPLOYMENT, CANADA, 1961−1979
(percentage increase over each 5-year period)

Period	Labour Force	Clerical Employment
1961−1965	19.4	19.5
1966−1970	20.4	23.4
1971−1975	23.8	33.4
1975−1979	19.8	12.0

Source: Clerical employment data from Statistics Canada (1980*a*). Labour force data from Statistics Canada (1978*a*, 1979*a*, 1979*b*, 1980*c*).

survey indicated that these women are now seeking to obtain greater authority in their jobs. Girls from less-well-to-do homes, however, were still thinking along the lines of more traditional female work, with their ambitions for responsibility limited to supervisory work.

Two other recent attitude surveys (Porter *et al.*, 1979; Russell, 1978) indicate a persistence of orientation toward traditional female work requiring few skills and little responsibility—in other words, toward jobs that fit traditional female stereotypes. These two studies strongly suggest that a majority of the women entering the work-force over the next decade or so will continue seeking and equipping themselves for employment in clerical, sales, and service occupations.

Older women returning to the labour market also tend to find employment in traditional female occupations. From 1976 to 1979, the proportion of women re-entrants falling into the clerical, sales, and service ranks remained relatively unchanged at about two thirds of all women re-entrants.

This combination of occupational segregation plus inertia makes it all the more important to study the employment effects of informatics before the new technology reaches the take-off point of rapid diffusion. If informatics has a negative impact on clerical-type information handling and related jobs, as has been forecast in numerous studies,[3] women might require special assistance in order to ensure that what should be simply a mobility problem does not deteriorate into a crisis of structural unemployment.

Chapter Two will provide a brief introduction to the so-called ''office of the future.'' It will discuss the forces bringing it about, describe the technological developments behind it, explore some of the forms it is taking, and review some existing examples representing its different phases and forms.

NOTES

[1] For current data from the monthly labour force survey, see various issues of Statistics Canada (1980c). For historical data, see Dominion Bureau of Statistics (1967b), which gives figures from the old labour force series for 1953–1966, and Statistics Canada (1979a), which gives data from the new labour force series for 1966–1978.

[2] For the census labour force data, see Dominion Bureau of Statistics (1967a), Statistics Canada (1975), and Statistics Canada (1978b). Note that female labour force participation rates based on the labour force surveys are typically several points higher than those shown in the census, for both married and single women.

[3] Published estimates range up to 30 or 40 per cent unemployment in these areas. The studies on which such figures are based are critically reviewed in a recent report by the Institute for Research on Public Policy to the Department of Communications (Zeman, 1979).

Chapter Two

The Office of the Future: What's in It?

Chapter One looked at women in the labour force and found them not only concentrated in a handful of occupations, such as clerical work, but also likely to remain in such segregated occupations even as they increase their labour-force participation through the 1980s and 1990s. This chapter will look at the new technology—informatics—which is transforming not only the jobs these women do but also the entire environment in which they work.

The new environment has been variously labelled the "office of the future," the "electronic office," and the "automated office." In strictly technological terms, all of the labels refer to a situation in which a whole range of informatics equipment—such as word processors and facsimile machines, backed by computer power—have been or will be introduced into an office environment. In organizational terms, the office of the future implies streamlining and standardizing the flow of work-related information, as well as the jobs associated with the gathering, processing, composition, storage, retrieval, and communication of that information. In corporate management terms, it means greater effectiveness for decision makers and greater productivity for office workers.

The push for office productivity has both accelerated the movement toward the office of the future, and at least indirectly, helped to shape it. When business reported in the late 1970s that office costs had doubled over the previous ten years to represent as much as 50 per cent of some organizations' overhead, and yet that productivity had risen a mere 4 per cent in office work compared to 80 per cent in manufacturing, the lines of battle were drawn.

There was an implied lesson from the intense capitalization of manufacturing over the previous decades. One United States study (Young, 1978) reported that the average white-collar worker is supported by only $2,000 in capital investment, compared to $25,000 in capital investment for every worker in manufacturing. There was also a built-in prejudice in productivity indices toward what could most easily be measured—such as information recording and other clerical work rather than the more value-added information work of, say, market analysis.

So the most obvious target for increased productivity was seen as the huge paperburden of office work. One consulting firm (WPI, 1977), for instance, estimated that the average office worker is supported by between six and ten cubic feet of filing. Further, it estimated that between 20 and 30 per cent of professionals' and executives' time is lost while either searching or waiting for information to be retrieved from those files.

From the beginning, the computer has been used as an office-productivity aid—for instance, for maintaining inventory, pay-roll, and other numerical records. The effect has been to reduce the number of low-skilled clerical positions and create new jobs for computer-specialists while substituting print-outs for record books.

The so-called "automated office" entails the use of both computer and telecommunications technology, which together enable the processing and storing as well as the transmission of information. This information can be words and graphics as well as numerical data. Hence, the office of the future touches the lives of far more than just number-crunching specialists and ledger-keeping clerks.

For instance, some desk-top terminals feature not only electronic agendas, but also "ticklers" to remind executives of reports due either by them or to them. Electronic messages bypass receptionists as well as the mail system. Word processors and text editors take the retyping out of typing and even the typesetting away from typesetters. Facsimile printers allow for remote photocopying within the office or across the country. Magnetic tapes and disks complement or replace manila files, filing cabinets, and file clerks.

Some word processors are stand-alone units capable only of processing instructions and storing information locally. Others are time shared; they derive their logic power from a central computer shared with other word processors. Still others are communicating word processors, capable of sending and receiving material, as well as processing and storing it.

Beneath all the jargon associated with the office of the future, the process of change and the operating technology are fairly easily explained. The process involves the automation of information-handling work functions, not only in the office itself but wherever else information handling goes on—in warehouses, supermarkets, and even in factories and mines. While this type of work is most heavily concentrated in the tertiary or service sector of the economy (Valaskakis, 1979, p. 29), what is coming to be known as the "information sector" takes in part of the work involved in the primary (resources) and secondary (manufacturing) sectors as well. This is so simply because the nature of the part of the work in those sectors involves dealing with abstract information content, rather than concrete material products.

The process of automating information work begins with the installation of basic computer and communications equipment, which can be upgraded over time—if, that is, the equipment is compatible, and if a fully integrated electronic office is the ultimate goal. As it progresses, the process increasingly removes information from a paper mode and puts it into an electronic medium.

Even the most complicated of automated office equipment can be understood in terms of three basic component parts: logic, memory, and input-output. Most of the equipment now being sold became commercially feasible only after the invention of the microprocessor in 1972, which brought the power and price range of computers forward from a relatively small and specialized user community to an immensely larger general-purpose market.

The microprocessor is essentially a computer on a chip. It consists of one or a set of large-scale integrated circuits called micro-electronic "chips," which can perform the basic logic functions of a larger computer's central processing unit, but at a fraction of the cost. In a word processor, for instance, microprocessors allow the operator to change the order of paragraphs around on the screen, and to have the revised copy stored in memory. Happily, the size of microprocessors is decreasing, their capacity is increasing (the number of components per chip is said to be doubling every year), and their price is tumbling.

Other basic components of information equipment include memory and interface. Memory chips hold information in electronic form; a state-of-the-art chip will hold up to a quarter of a million binary digits (bits) of information, which is enough to store many pages of text. Up until recently, costs were falling at about 40 per cent per year (although this is apparently no longer the case).

There are numerous modes of memory, each of which is associated with a different speed of access and unit cost. Solid-state or on-line memory is the most expensive but most speedily accessed. Traditionally, information was stored on magnetic tapes or disks. New forms of storage include bubble memory, which although it is much faster, resembles magnetic tape in that it is "non-volatile" (which is to say that the information is not lost when the power is turned off). Recent advances in video-disk, optical-storage technology also appear to offer fast, inexpensive, and reliable memory along with massive capacity: a single disk is said to be able to store the complete contents of the *Encyclopaedia Britannica*, at a fraction of the cost of conventional electronic storage.

Finally, there are input-output chips that allow the microprocessor unit within, say, an electronic cash register, to "interface" or communicate with the outside world. The outside world can be a telecopier, a facsimile machine, or another computer or terminal. The communicating medium can be any of the existing networks, such as telephone lines, television cables, or satellite relay stations.

The closer integration and greater accessibility of these electronic technologies have meant that business information is being increasingly created, stored, and used electronically, and that more information-handling work can now be performed automatically.

An early example of informatics on public display was the airlines' use of computer terminals in their local offices and at airport counters. At first the terminal's microprocessor capacity was used simply to book a customer's seat from the inventory, which was accessed via a leased-line connection to the airline's central computer. Today, the capacity of both the central computer and the local terminal allow for ticket and boarding-pass printing, parts and aircraft inventory control, and detailed market analysis.

Another less obvious pioneer in informatics was the telephone industry. The experience of this industry is worth exploring, not only for possible insights related to employment repercussions, but because this industry, as a partner in the computer and communications complex, could impart a distinct direction or approach to the development of informatics in Canada.

The major informatics innovations in the modern telephone industry are electronic switching and stored-programme control. Together, they have enabled more and more long-distance call switching to be done automatically. They have also greatly reduced the work of installation and maintenance, since the complicated wiring associated with traditional electro-mechanical equipment has been replaced by simplified solid-state electronic components. However, since work such as connecting and recording billing data on long-distance phone calls relates more directly to the type of work functions examined in this study, the installation-related service work will be ignored in favour of the information-handling work itself.

Adapting the computer's stored programme capacity to do the work of connecting phone lines for local and long-distance calling, electronic switching systems (ESS) increase the speed of service and the capacity of the system. In the United States, where electronic switching systems were introduced for local calls in 1965 and for long distance in 1976, call-handling capacities are estimated to have increased threefold for local and fourfold for long-distance calls handled by the electronic switching systems (U.S. Bureau of Labor Statistics, 1979). One reason for this is that the operator's involvement has been substantially reduced.

In Canada, the new, semi-automated or semi-self-service long-distance system is called "traffic operator position system" (TOPS). Under this system, the operator no longer handles a whole call but only part of it—the customer's billing instructions—and that only on the minority of calls still requiring operator assistance. After dialing, the connection is made automatically; billing information is collected and relayed to the accounting department automatically. Since the introduction of the traffic operator position system to Toronto in 1978, the number of operators has been reduced by 40 per cent (Kuyek, 1979, p. 67). According to officials with the Communications Workers of Canada, a further staff reduction of 20 to 25 per cent is anticipated when mechanized directory assistance is introduced some time in 1981.

The threat to women's jobs in the telephone industry is clear. Women represent over 90 per cent of telephone operators and a similarly high proportion of other clerical workers and related supervisory personnel (Statistics Canada, 1980*a*).

The introduction of the traffic operator position system has effectively eliminated jobs in some rural centres (such as in the interior of British Columbia), as the long-distance operators' work is consolidated and centralized using fewer operators. But in addition to the outright elimination of jobs, there are subtler and more indirect effects of telephone informatics. One of the most important is that the skill content of jobs is being changed. Some jobs, such as long-distance operators under the traffic operator position system, have been deskilled, even trivialized (Kuyek, 1979, p. 69). Others, for instance in translating and analysing network operating data, are becoming increasingly complex and demanding (U.S. Bureau of Labor Statistics, 1979, p. 30).

In some cases, informatics is also replacing supervisory personnel with computer monitoring and instant feedback on productivity. This is happening in long-distance operator work as well as with customer-service office work (Kuyek, 1979, p. 69).

The great range of sometimes contradictory employment effects of informatics in the telephone industry alone should illustrate the danger of generalizing ''the'' work impact of this ubiquitous yet enigmatic technology. It might be possible, though, to identify some general patterns—for instance, a pattern of job elimination in highly standardized and single-function job areas, or a pattern of work consolidation or shifting skill requirements in other information-type work.

In the four case studies that follow, some common elements and themes do surface. The first case study examines the impact of informatics on a large corporate head office typical of such offices in Canada. The second case study explores the implementation of informatics in a major Canadian insurance company, a process that came about as an extension of the company's already sophisticated data-processing system and related computer capacity. The third and fourth case studies adopt a wider focus, examining the overall trends of informatics innovation and employment shifts within the finance and retail trade industries.

Although all the companies and industries examined are at the leading edge of a change process so vast and dynamic that the trends they are setting might eventually be reversed, there appears to be at least a polarization of approach that can be described with some certainty. The two approaches are what this report will call *télématique* and *privatique*. Although the terms were first used in connection with the Nora-Minc report, *The Computerization of Society*, prepared for the President of France (Nora and Minc, 1978, 1980), they will not be used here in the strict sense of their original meaning.

Télématique, as described in the Nora-Minc report, envisages a vast electronic highway or utility accessible to anyone anywhere in the world for any conceivable information-based purpose. The term *privatique* is taken from the notion put forward by two dissenters to the Nora-Minc report (Lussato and Bounine, 1979). They maintain that the integration of computer and communications technology will not necessarily lead to a single global network, but could produce a diffusion of many independent informatics loci, each with its own computer power and having relatively little need for communications with central computers or giant data bases in remote locations. Hence the term *privatique*.

The *télématique* scenario developed in the Nora-Minc report arose from a focus on the enabling technology itself. By extension, it is possible that the *télématique* approach will triumph where corporate planners concentrate on and try to exploit the full capabilities of the new technology, or where the corporate personalities involved in the process of change (such as managers and engineers in the data processing and information systems departments) are themselves creatures of the initial phases of informatics development.

It appears, for instance, that the data-processing and information systems personnel created in the first phase of informatics—computerization—tend to focus more on the process of obtaining the information required for decision making in a large corporate office and, accordingly, lean toward the *télématique* approach with its stress on system and process rather than content. On the other hand, the administrative services personnel, who traditionally administer the strictly office functions of a company, seem to regard information more as an end in itself and, accordingly, tend to acquire informatics systems specifically geared to their unique and private purposes.

Interestingly, a systems analyst interviewed for this study used a pipeline metaphor and the image of continuous information flows to illustrate the *télématique* nature of his work. Another, who previously helped to develop what he described as an ''electronic utility'' for meeting the company's information-processing needs, now talks of plugging into it other ''appliances,'' such as copier machines and typewriters.

There are profound implications to each of these two different approaches. The *privatique* approach suggests that informatics will be implemented in a diffused manner with each corporation and corporate department relatively free to design its own system. The *télématique* approach seems linked to a more centralized process, with a master plan being implemented either from the top down or from the bottom up. The suggested scope and pace of change differ as well. Under the *privatique* approach, the traditional office seems to remain, although its support equipment and job functions are transformed to the electronic mode—for instance, through the purchase of stand-alone word-processing equipment. On the other hand, the *télématique* orientation would favour automating all information-related office functions and integrating them within a multi-functional decision-making support system, held together by a company-wide, electronic communications network.

It is also possible that the presence of a strong communications network such as that which already exists in Canada could itself encourage a *télématique* approach emphasizing infrastructure, rather than content. This possibility would become even more probable if the specialization of this country's communications capacity became a matter of policy—in an attempt to ensure Canada's stake in the office of the future.

History will reveal the winning pattern. It will also make or break the reputation of the many consultants and soothsayers speculating as to when the office of the future will enter the present tense.

Table 2.1 summarizes a recent study of the market penetration of informatics and related equipment in Canada. Comparing the number of word processors with the total number of office typewriters, it seems that informatics has not even achieved the 10 per cent market penetration that many consultants had been estimating for large companies in Canadian urban centres by mid-1980. On the other hand, as the previous discussion on the *télématique* versus the *privatique* approach points out, what constitutes office automation can often depend on the perspective of the observer. For instance, if it is perceived as merely a little additional software added into what was originally a data-processing system, the assessment on informatics diffusion might be greater than if the observer was counting only strictly office-equipment-related, special-purpose informatics technology.

Until now, the diffusion of informatics equipment has not reached the point where cost-benefit feedback has started accelerating the process. However, the electronic infrastructure already in place (telephones, electric typewriters, computer equipment and systems) could be considered to be exerting a certain technological push. Further investments offer compound

Table 2.1
OFFICE AUTOMATION EQUIPMENT IN CANADA, 1978

Type of Equipment	Number of Units[a]
Business telephones	4,500,000
Office typewriters	800,000
Non-communicating word processors	18,000
Communicating word processors	1,000
Computers	18,000
Data terminals	250,000
Telex, TWX, and other message terminals	56,000
Facsimile terminals	8,000
Photocopy machines	300,000

Note: a. Estimated.
Source: From a survey done for the Department of Communications (Hough, 1980).

benefits at relatively small additional cost. In addition, one of the major economic deterrents to informatics—the high cost of electronic storage—is expected to disappear soon as the cost of disk files drops. Finally, voice-based electronic mail and other systems may become commercially viable by the late 1980s (Cirrito *et al.*, 1980).

Still, the decision to invest in the technology will depend, during much of the 1980s, on factors outside the technology itself. Here are some of the factors influencing that choice:

- As already mentioned, the hope that capital investment in the office may be the key to unlocking much-needed productivity increases there is one compelling factor.
- Also helping to push new investment is the widespread industry concern that without substantial productivity increases, Canada could face a labour shortage by the late 1980s.
- Rising energy costs will undoubtedly accelerate the diffusion process. Teleconferencing and electronic mail will gradually replace business meetings and ordinary mail.
- Increased business competition both within Canada and around the world will require more efficient operations. Informatics promises to provide the key through more sophisticated control over all aspects related to the information content of those operations.
- As another possible accelerating factor, the Canadian government is already financially committed to promoting informatics—through its support of Telidon (two-way television) and of AES, a word-processing system manufacturer that is now a Crown corporation—as well as through its $12.5 million programme for developing the office of the future.
- Other government-related factors, however, could slow down the diffusion process. For instance, there is no policy regarding the difference between telecommunications carriers and business services related to telecommunications. Pending policy clarification, businesses might be leery to proceed.
- Similarly, unions might resist the further diffusion of video-display terminals until such time as their concerns relating to possible radiation and vision problems have been satisfactorily resolved.
- Concerns for personal privacy might also retard the diffusion of electronic funds transfer systems (EFTS).

In evaluating the various factors affecting the rate of diffusion of informatics technology, it is safe to assume that the factors tending to accelerate it outweigh the factors tending to slow it down. It is possible that by 1986, the diffusion rate could be such that the average company in the service sector will have reached the point of informatics maturity, which the companies to be examined in Chapters Three and Four—companies on the leading edge of change—had already reached in 1977.

Certainly, as this chapter has demonstrated, Canada is entering a period of profound technological change. The electronics-based office of the future, based on the melding of computers and telecommunications, promises to alter vastly the way in which business-related information and the information business are handled. Some of the employment effects of these changes will be illustrated in the four case studies that follow.

It has already been pointed out that with the advent of microprocessors, businesses concerned with the handling of information have gained an inexpensive, versatile, and increasingly "friendly" tool. In combining variations on that tool into what is known as the office of the future, there are two main approaches, each with distinctly different implications.

In the first of the case studies to follow, the company taken as the example is following one of these approaches—the *télématique* approach.

Chapter Three

Case Study: A Large Corporate Head Office

The previous chapter charted the bewildering new territory of the office of the future, demystifying the jargon, explaining some basic concepts, and identifying alternative approaches. This chapter offers the first of two company case studies on office automation in Canada. It describes the specific forms of informatics technology involved, the process whereby these are being introduced, and the effects this process is having on the company's work and people.

The company chosen for the first case study is a large, well-established, and broadly diversified Canadian corporation. Principally engaged in the transportation and communications sector, the company is one of Canada's largest employers, and has annual revenues exceeding several billion dollars. This case study examines what happened when office automation was introduced into the company's head office.

THE TECHNOLOGY

Although the general types of electronic equipment involved in the automation of this typical large office have already been described in the previous chapter, a brief summary might help to differentiate this exclusively *office* automation equipment from the rest of the informatics line.

Word-processing machines combine the mechanical features of a typewriter with the logic features of a microprocessor (computer on a chip). The word processor enables its operator to enter a preliminary version of a text (letter, contract, manuscript, etc.), and then to eliminate unwanted passages, move paragraphs around, and finally store the text for future use. Numerous additional features are available on some lines of word-processing equipment and related software, including features for editing and typesetting (text-editing machines), for sending or receiving text or graphic material (communicating word processors), and for electronic mail (capabilities such as automatically targeting mail to selected people). It should also be noted that almost any computer terminal can become a word processor if the appropriate software is used.

Facsimile transmission refers to the process of transmitting texts and illustrations electronically—usually via the telephone using a telecopier.

When the material to be transmitted is already in electronic form, any communicating word processor can do this job, but when only a paper copy is available, a facsimile machine must be used to transmit the actual visual image of the document.

Electronic filing is a somewhat exotic term that suggests a complete transformation of information into instantly accessible electronic bit form. There are, in fact, a range of information storage forms, with the most cumbersome though cheapest being only slightly more exciting than a drawer full of manila file folders. Each type of storage or memory differs in form, cost, and the time it takes to get the information into or out of the "file." Reels of magnetic tape, which require serial access, are slow but inexpensive; stacks of magnetic disks allow random access and are thus faster, but more expensive; on-line memory is the fastest of all, but the quantity that can be stored is limited, and it is also the most expensive form of storage.

THE PROCESS OF AUTOMATION

As seems to be typical at least among companies at the leading edge of informatics innovation, the computer-sired data-processing department played an important role as catalyst of this corporation's transition into office automation.

As it gathered more and more data and stored it electronically, the head office's data-processing division developed discrete data bases, and over time, integrated these with a tele-processing network. As its capacity to synthesize data from different sources grew, and as it increased the capacity of the original system (from basic computing to comparative analysis and even chart preparation), the distinction between what it could do and what other departments were doing not only blurred but was eliminated. A name change was in order—from data processing to information systems.

Five years later, the first of an increasingly prolific line of office automation equipment was being introduced by other departments engaged in office work. The department most traditionally concerned with the office itself—administrative services—undertook, perhaps as its rightful duty, to oversee the company's initiation into the use of this equipment.

After a staff reorganization along government-approved lines of demarcation, which in effect divided secretarial functions between word-processor operator and administrative assistant (Coopers, Currie and Lybrand Ltd., 1980), the administrative services department established work stations where the word-processor operators handled the centralized typing requirements of that department as well as special requests—such as report writing—from other departments. Then in 1979, the department launched a pilot facsimile transmission service to the company's regional offices.

The introduction of office automation equipment by the administrative services department was paralleled by the development of main-frame computer-based word-processing capacity in the information systems (formerly data processing) department. This overlapping of efforts finally came to senior management's attention, and a possible struggle for dominance in the new field of office automation was averted only when the company president commissioned an interdepartmental study group to look into the question. The group completed a series of cost-benefit studies and concluded that office automation was imperative. It drafted a master plan many times larger in scope than the automation of text handling, file storage, and information distribution functions, which had characterized the initial efforts of the administrative services department.

The plan of the interdepartmental study group called for a telecommunications grid connecting senior corporate desks with regional and local offices. Its capacity was to include interactive reporting, remote and personal computing, facsimile document and graphics transmission, and electronic memo and message sending. Its operating units—desk-top terminals—were to feature appointment calendars, electronic files with personalized index, electronic word- and text-processing capacity, plus access to various corporate data bases.

The objective envisaged was twofold: to increase the effectiveness of the decision-making staff, and to eliminate the costlier aspects of running the head office. Some excerpts from the cost-benefit studies illustrate the extent of change envisaged over the ten years of the master plan, launched in 1980.

In an analysis of filing and paper costs, the study group found that the company's head office harboured 53 million sheets of paper and that this quantity was increasing at roughly 9 per cent a year. For space alone, the storage costs amounted to a quarter of a million dollars a year, and this was increasing at a rate of 2.5 per cent a year, since the pace of purging paper was not keeping up with the growth of fresh input. The labour required was equal to that of fifty full-time filing clerks, or 104,000 person-hours a year, presumably growing at a rate of 9 per cent a year.

As files moved into an electronic form, or the cheaper microfiche form, not only paper was saved but time and space as well. One executive using microfiched records can now lay his hands on information within thirty seconds, whereas it used to take him five minutes or more to locate and extract the same material from the appropriate file. Having the files collapsed in microfiche form and thus within easy reach of the executive at his desk has also meant relief from the lengthy search and wait processes. Further, it allows for more unassisted searching, checking, and cross-referencing.

The company's mail survey found that 70 per cent of internally generated outgoing mail was destined for elsewhere within the corporate network and, further, that copies of original correspondence represented over a third of that total. It was this core of internal correspondence that was identified as an obvious initial candidate for conversion to electronic mail.

In addition to this core of intracompany outgoing mail, the study found that 55 per cent of incoming mail originated within the corporate network as well. As branch offices are gradually plugged into the corporation's electronic information network, this 55 per cent of incoming mail will also begin moving by electronic means.

Interestingly, the interdepartmental study devoted relatively little time to analysing secretaries' time, or to the potential savings to be made through the installation of simple word-processing work stations.

EMPLOYMENT EFFECTS

Office automation has profoundly altered employment in the information services department to which it has been most fully introduced. As Figure 3.1 illustrates, there has been a sharp reversal in the ratio of clerical-support information workers to professional and managerial information workers. This reduction in the clerical category accompanied a major expansion in the department's activities; yet the additional labour demand was confined to the professional and managerial ranks.

At first there was simply a reduction in new clerical job openings. Eventually, though, the reduction in clerical labour demand exceeded the natural attrition rate. The department moved some personnel to clerical positions in other departments, with a few even accepting demotions to fit in. None was laid off, however.

Of critical importance to the employment equation, it should be noted that only 2 of the 130 workers displaced from the clerical ranks moved up to the professional or managerial ranks. This bears out the finding of a 1978 study for the Department of Industry, Trade and Commerce (Peitchinis, 1978, p. 147) of skill requirements and technological change, to the effect that technological changes would increasingly require that workers possess greater technical knowledge, above and beyond those skills that can be acquired relatively quickly and through on-the-job training. In other words, the problem is becoming not just one of step-by-step job mobility, but rather one of complete occupational discontinuity.

Phrased yet another way, this finding raises the concern that informatics is disproportionately reducing the labour content of low-skilled or clerical-level information occupations, while increasing the skill content of professional information work. This would mean that entry-level job requirements might rise faster than the natural evolution of work-force skills and aptitude, with the would-be clerical workers plus the eventually displaced office workers becoming potentially unemployable. Further, if employment growth continues to favour occupations requiring higher professional qualifications, while informatics continues to reduce employment in, say, the mailroom, administrative services, and other departments, the lateral-transfer option could eventually be exhausted.

Figure 3.1

CLERICAL AND PROFESSIONAL EMPLOYMENT IN THE INFORMATION SERVICES OF A LARGE CORPORATION, 1972 AND 1980

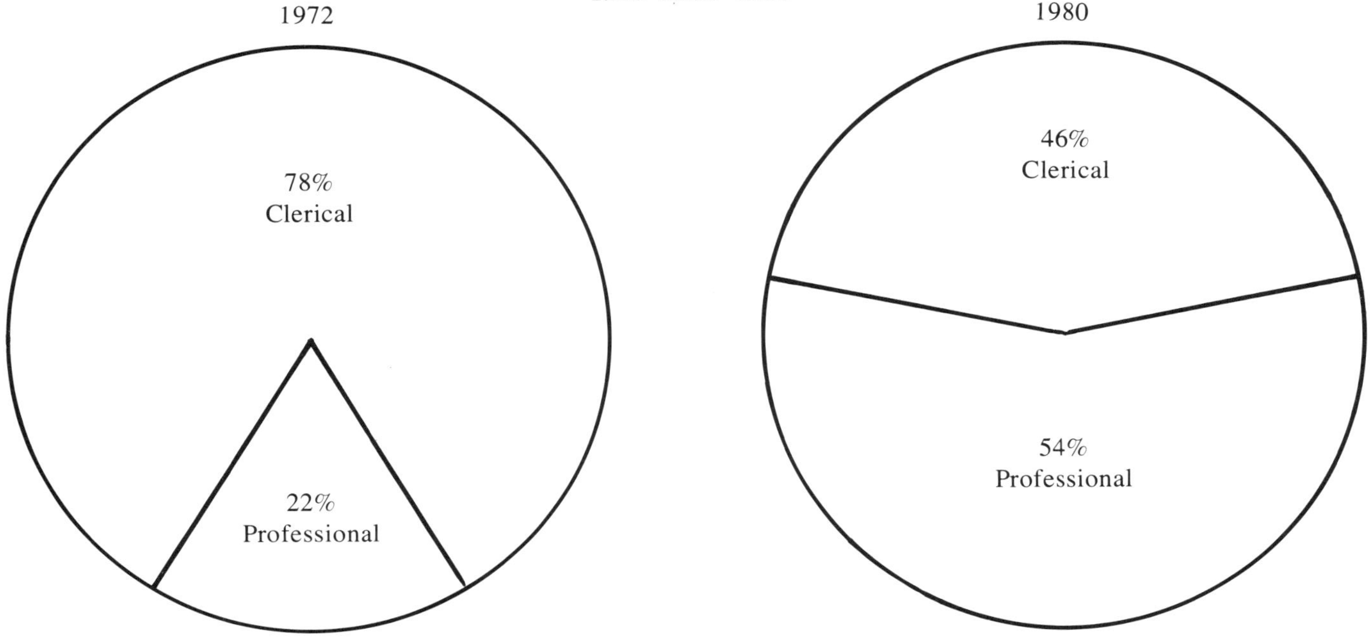

1972

78% Clerical

22% Professional

1980

46% Clerical

54% Professional

Note: Over the eight-year period from 1972 to 1980, total employment in the information services department declined by 10 per cent.

Source: Personal communication to the author from the company's personnel department.

Among women workers, the 25 women in the 200-strong professional and management group of 1980 were indeed a marked improvement over the 2 lone females of 1972. However, these 25 women represented only a quarter of the 100 women displaced from clerical employment during the period. Furthermore, none of those 100 was in fact able to move up into the professional ranks.

In the strictly secretarial aspects of office work, between 6 and 8 word-processor operators in two work stations take care of all the text-handling requirements of all but 2 of the 200 members of the professional and managerial group. Only 2 of the top 50 personnel still have their own secretaries. These secretaries are now more appropriately described as administrative assistants, although the company has not gone as far as IBM, which has transformed the administrative assistant position into a training ground for senior management. Nonetheless, it is clear that the clerical aspects of traditional secretarial functions have shrunk to a small fraction of what they used to be. Savings have come about in several ways, as described below.

By the end of their first year's exposure to the automated equipment's potential, managers with terminals of their own (50 in this department) are getting used to using the keyboard themselves, thereby reducing not only their use of paper, but also their need for someone else to convert handwritten or dictated communications into typed form. One manager estimates that 50 per cent of what he used to send on paper he now sends electronically, and on his own. Most of the other 49 executives in the department who have terminals also use them themselves, although not all have managed such a great reduction in their use of paper.

Retyping work, which is estimated to comprise up to 70 per cent of typing time, is also substantially reduced. In one example, two senior executives used their computer terminals to confer on the drafting of a corporate policy document. Exchanging updates on a single draft three times before finalizing the content, they saved themselves and their secretaries six paper versions of the text. They also saved themselves and their secretaries the time and tedium of finding mutually convenient meeting times. Also eliminated were photocopying time and material costs, plus the cost and lost time of transporting the drafts between the two offices. The secreatary took over only at the end, correcting spelling mistakes and punctuation, designing the layout and, finally, instructing the word-processing unit to produce the required number of copies at the required locations.

A number of changes in secretarial work have been identified. There is a reduction in the need for traditional skills—for instance, in good layout and correct hyphenation, both of which used to come from long experience. There is also less need for typing accuracy, since corrections are as simple as backing up the cursor and retyping. In addition, shorthand skills dry up as the experience of using a computer terminal seems to help break down the long-standing antipathy to dictating equipment, which has kept those useful machines off to the side of offices, gathering dust, and used only 10 per cent of the time according to some industry studies (WPI, 1977), despite their availability since the 1940s.

Figure 3.2 demonstrates the collapsing nature of traditional secretarial work as evidenced in this study. The circle graph on the right offers a hypothetical breakdown of the secretary's (or administrative assistant's) use of time in the office of the future, based on the trends evolving in the office studied here. It suggests more value-added job functions—such as in research assignments, finding and analysing information for briefings, and so forth. It also suggests that a different set of skills will be required, such as better human relations skills for helping to get the research done, as well as more general and technical knowledge.

As the following chapter will reveal, the countervailing skill effects of informatics are not limited to the large corporate head office, which was the subject of our first case study, but show up in information occupations in the insurance industry as well.

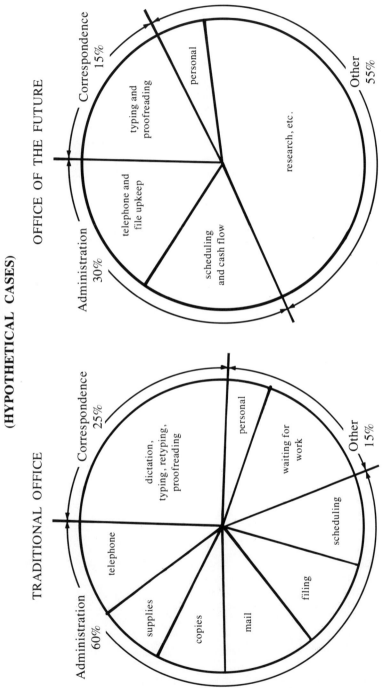

Figure 3.2
JOB CONTENT OF SECRETARIAL WORK BEFORE AND AFTER OFFICE AUTOMATION (HYPOTHETICAL CASES)

TRADITIONAL OFFICE

OFFICE OF THE FUTURE

Chapter Four

Case Study: A Major Insurance Company

In the company described in the previous chapter, one might expect that the employment effects of informatics would be largely confined to those departments—in particular, data processing and administrative services—where handling information represents a large component of the work involved. But with most of the work in line departments falling outside the theoretical boundaries of what is coming to be known as the "information sector," the impact of informatics on overall employment in the company should be much less.

In the insurance industry, though, information work accounts for 90 per cent of all employment. Hence, informatics could be expected to touch nearly every department in one way or another, with the eventual effects going far beyond that which might be expected from strictly office automation in other industries. The result could be no less than a transformation of the entire shape of this predominantly information-oriented industry.

Insurance is a sizeable industry in Canada, contributing $1.1 billion to the gross domestic product in 1979, up 50 per cent since 1971. It has also been a major source of employment growth over the last twenty years, particularly for women. However, over the last five years, employment

Table 4.1
FEMALE EMPLOYMENT IN INSURANCE CARRIERS, CANADA, 1975 AND 1980[a]

Job Category	Female Employment		Change from 1975–1980	Females/Total Employment (both sexes) in Job Category, 1980	Females in Job Category/ All Females in Insurance, 1980
	1975	1980			
Clerical	50,000	44,000	−6,000 (−12%)	90%	71%
Managerial and Professional	6,000	5,000	−1,000 (−17%)	29%	8%
All Job Categories[b]	63,000	62,000	−1,000 (−2%)	59%	100%

Note: a. June 1975 and June 1980.
      b. Includes job categories not shown above.
Source: From unpublished data supplied by the Labour Force Survey Division (Statistics Canada, 1980a).

33

growth has lagged considerably, and even declined for women. Employment in insurance carriers increased by 20 per cent during the 1960s, but by only 14 per cent during the 1970s.

As Table 4.1 demonstrates, overall employment in the industry increased a mere 6 per cent during the latter half of the 1970s, and female employment actually decreased by 2 per cent. Still, in 1980, women represented over half of all employment in insurance carriers, and 71 per cent of those women were in clerical occupations.

While the case study does not conclusively demonstrate a causal link between informatics and the negative growth of employment among female insurance-carrier workers, the employment insights provided at least make it difficult to discount such an association.

The company chosen for the case study is a major insurance carrier principally involved in individual life insurance. Employing over a thousand people in Canada, and with assets of several billion dollars, it is one of this country's ten largest companies in that line of business.

THE TECHNOLOGY

While most of the equipment and work processes involved in this insurance company's three-phase implementation of informatics are already familiar, there are a few specialized applications worth mentioning.

Batch processing is a form of computerized data handling particularly geared to bulk information manipulation requirements that arise when dealing with thousands of insurance premiums. Similar data items are grouped together and processed during a single machine run with the same programme.

If an insurance branch office is *on-line*, it is hooked up to the company's central computer, and probably has direct access to the company's computerized data bases. This means that insurance operations can be performed immediately, thereby avoiding the delays associated with *off-line* transactions.

Data banks are comprehensive, non-redundant, and structured sets of data that are organized independently of their applications and are readily accessible for further use. Electronic data in themselves do not necessarily represent a data bank; first, such data have to be organized and integrated into an appropriate format.

THE PROCESS OF AUTOMATION

In the *first phase* of information automation or informatics, the company acquired computer capacity and set up a data-processing department. Its work was to gather, process, and store data on the financial transactions flowing through the corporate network. From simply maintaining data files, the department developed an ever-extending data bank network that provided data support services to other departments, beginning with the strictly numerically oriented departments such as those associated with cost accounting.

In the *second phase* of informatics implementation, electronically based information became accessible to more decision makers and professionals throughout the company. In addition, these people became increasingly able to access that information themselves. Not only were the data on-line, but the programmes needed to make use of them were now simple enough to employ, so that specialized computer programmers were no longer necessary as intermediaries between the user and the data.

Accompanying this phase, the company underwent a major reorganization. Whole departments were realigned according to their task content, with like tasks amalgamated under one central authority. As a result, the data-processing department was merged with the administrative services department, bringing mail room, printing, inventory and supplies, records, and copying all under the same management as that of the various computer services. Office work was also reorganized, with administrative work stations set up to handle, as separate tasks, typing, telephone answering, and administrative assistance.

The stage was set for the *third phase*—the automation of specific work functions. Building on the on-line capacity and experience gained in the previous two phases of informatics implementation, the company was able to bring about far-reaching efficiencies with a fairly small additional investment. For example, when equipment for office automation was introduced as part of the third phase, it took the form of extra capacity added on to the already existing computer-based system. The effects of these changes were exponential, enhancing the company's overall operations, not just its office work.

Some of the work functions included in the third phase of informatics implementation include preparation of insurance promotional material, issuing and processing premiums, monitoring birthdays, and even basic underwriting.

Traditionally, insurance agents staked their reputations on remembering clients' birthdays far enough in advance to be able to encourage them to upgrade their insurance coverage before the rates went up (on their birthday, of course). Now, thanks to the informatics advances in this company, a computer programme monitors all birth dates in all policyholders' files, and triggers the automatic production of a "personalized" letter promoting additional insurance coverage, which, after completion by the word processor, is sent directly to the client. Not only is the agent relieved of this work, but the branch office support staff is also relieved of many filing, file-monitoring, and letter-writing tasks, which are now completely unnecessary. Similarly, changes of address can be handled directly at the head office, where optical scanners are able to do most of the work.

The automation of premium billing and payment handling has reduced the total amount of labour required for these functions. Work from a series of often repetitious tasks performed by many different persons has been reduced to what is sometimes simply one short human intervention. Not only are premium notices sent out automatically—using boilerplate or stock paragraphs—but often the premiums themselves are even collected automatically, by electronic funds transfer. In such cases, payment of the premium is by direct debit from the policyholder's bank account.

The effect of automated billing has been the elimination of one complete clerical function in the branch, that of cash accounting. The remittance-processing function at head office has also been eliminated.

In 1980, the company began automating the issue-writing aspect of underwriting insurance. A rather specialized form of information work, writing the issue involves calculating what premium the individual must pay depending on his or her age and other factors. By applying the best analytical software to the wealth of data on insurance holders, the company's computer programmers drafted a set of parameters for risk and wrote a computer programme model for handling the underwriting requirements of all but the most exceptional clients. Increasingly, the underwriter only has to work on the difficult cases; this suggests that the amount of stress on underwriters may increase substantially, even as the total work-load decreases.

What is more, the automated system is expected to reduce clerical support staff engaged in underwriting (collating data, searching records, preparing forms), and even to reduce the demand for underwriters of group insurance. The company expects to increase its work volume in this category without increasing staff.

EMPLOYMENT EFFECTS

Even without speculating on the possible effects of the *fourth phase*, in which insurance will likely become more of a self-service business, the employment effects of the first three phases of informatics implementation in this insurance company have already been very great. In the future, in addition to ongoing advances in information-handling capacity, there will be constant refinements to the system, each one of which, to all appearances, will inexorably reduce labour requirements still further. For instance, when the more advanced (solid-state) forms of information storage replace the old-fashioned magnetic tapes and reels in the months ahead, seven tape librarians, whose job it has been to maintain and store those tapes, will be made redundant.

Nevertheless, it is potentially misleading to measure the employment effects of informatics simply in terms of jobs lost or gained. For instance, where a clerical worker leaves one branch office or department, that position might be terminated. In another branch, however, the manager might shift some of the customer-service work from the sales agents onto the office staff to compensate for the reduction in traditional clerical work without reducing staff. It is much more meaningful to measure the effects of informatics in terms of employment demand for particular occupations requiring certain skills, knowledge, and aptitude.

Among the direct effects observed, there has been a consistent reduction in clerical job functions associated with different insurance transactions. Examples include the centralization of client records and the automation of premium billing and some parts of client correspondence.

Another major and largely direct effect has been to reduce the labour content of insurance work, with most of that shrinkage concentrated, again, in the clerical component of that work. Examples range from the partial automation of word-processor-generated policy documents and promotional materials to the more recent moves toward automated underwriting. Here, routine issue writing, which could be construed to represent the clerical component of the underwriter's job, plus traditional clerical support functions, are being transformed from labour-intensive to capital-intensive operations.

Another major, though partially indirect, effect of informatics implementation in the insurance industry has been a reduction in the need for management personnel. Not only are there fewer people to manage for every routine aspect of insurance work, but the computer's built-in monitoring capability substitutes admirably for personal supervision. In addition, computer-aided instruction is reducing the teaching work that supervisory staff used to do from basic instruction to handling merely the difficult cases. As a result, the company now operates on a ratio of one instructor for fifteen staff, compared to one for five before computer-aided instruction was introduced.

This bears out the comment from one personnel officer with this insurance company that in terms of the number of employees at different skill levels, the shape of the company's employment profile is changing from a pyramid to a barrel. It also supports the finding of an earlier study of computers in insurance companies (Whisler, 1970) that first-line managers as well as clerical staff have been playing a diminishing role, both in terms of the scope of their work and in terms of their relative numbers compared to total employment in the industry.

Given women's comparatively recent breakthroughs into management positions, it is reasonable to assume that they would be concentrated in the lower-level management positions, and the company's personnel records bear this out.

Before getting into these statistics, two other general effects should be noted. The first is the indirect employment effects, such as the transfer of some traditionally ''sales'' work from the agents to office-based clerical workers. (An example would be following up by phone on the pre-birthday promotional pitch.) Such a transfer of functions might mask an otherwise even more serious erosion of clerical work in the company, and falsely imply that the technology was creating fresh information work at a clerical-skill level.

As was seen in the case of the increasing automation of underwriting, one of the effects of the new technology is to enable the company to increase its business *without* a proportionate increase in either professional or clerical staff. This second effect is called "jobless growth," and is a well-known phenomenon in highly capitalized primary and secondary industries, but as yet relatively rare in the tertiary sector. (For a discussion of jobless growth in industry, see Freeman 1977*a*.)

A related, though more indirect, effect—perhaps best described as a ripple effect, because it is so much more subtle—is the inherent potential of the informatics-mature company to expand into new insurance and other market areas, and to do this without an increase in staff commensurate with the employment it displaces elsewhere. By drawing away business from existing but more labour-intensive enterprises, the job losses would show up, not so much in the company or industry that successfully implemented informatics but in those companies and industries that failed to do so.

Finally, there are the subtle employment-related effects of the ongoing standardization, fragmentation, and separation of occupations and job functions. One company executive remarked in reference to the word-processor operators at remote work stations: "They don't even know who we are." That single comment speaks volumes about barriers to job mobility.

The company's personnel statistics bear out these generalized observations. While total employment rose by 260 in three years of informatics innovation ending June 1980, that growth was concentrated in the professional and specialist ranks. Over the course of that same three-year period, clerical workers' share of total employment declined by 12 per cent. On the other hand, specialist and professional employment increased by 10 per cent during the first nine months of 1979 alone.

In other words, during the 1970s, the company changed from a pillar of clerical employment to a pillar of professional and specialist employment. For the would-be clerical employee, the implications are bleak indeed, due to the marked reduction in new job openings. But while massive lay-offs of clerical workers would make headlines, failure to hire an equivalent number goes largely unnoticed. For the company, a smaller total work-force also implies a smaller recruitment and training pool from which to draw professional and management staff.

During the three-year period of informatics transformation discussed above, the average level of job complexity (measured on an industry index of "skill points") rose by 4 per cent. However, the number of compulsory job terminations (firings) also rose sharply to represent 41 per cent of total terminations during the first six months of 1980.

Exacerbating these difficulties, there appears to be a widening skills gap between what is considered clerical and what is considered professional work. Of the job openings posted internally during the first six months of 1980, only half resulted in internal candidates being chosen. The reason for this low internal promotion rate was, according to a company personnel official, ''the growing number of specialist positions demanding previous related experience.''

Recourse to outside candidates effectively aggravates the career discontinuity problem within the company by widening still further the skills gap between the professional and clerical levels. The trend might soon reach the point where the jobs for which demand is growing develop beyond the capacity of even the most earnest clerical worker to grow into, either by experience or through existing in-house training programmes. This means that the company would be increasingly dependent on external hirings. It would also leave the clerical workers in an extremely vulnerable position. Cut off from the option of upward mobility, their options for lateral mobility could also be exhausted if informatics continues to erode the company's requirements for clerical labour.

There is no evidence that this erosion of clerical jobs is slowing down; in fact, it may well be increasing. Of the remaining clerical-type jobs in the company, the majority are in decreasing demand, according to one company official. These jobs include tape librarians, discussed earlier, plus key-punch operators, data-entry clerks, group-pension clerks, suspense clerks (who monitor the flow of cheques), and even computer operators and junior data processors.

Although women do not form a majority of each of these job categories, they do represent the majority of clerical workers. In fact, as Table 4.1 indicates, they have even increased their share of the industry's overall clerical employment. But they hold a majority share of a rapidly declining job category. The already apparent decline in clerical employment in the insurance industry could push these women into unemployment, not as a result of lay-offs or firings, but due to lack of job openings in occupations for which they possess the necessary skills. In other words, they could well be unemployed by virtue of being out of joint with the times.

The next chapter will examine jobs of the future in banking.

Chapter Five

Case Study: Chartered Banks

Like the insurance industry described in the previous chapter, banking is highly information intensive, with financial information as the heart of its transaction-based work. One might expect, therefore, that the diffusion of informatics innovations among Canada's chartered banks would have similar employment effects.

In the company discussed in Chapter Four, these effects included the rationalization and amalgamation of jobs related to information handling and a parallel upgrading of occupational skill requirements for the average job recruit. While the focus of the previous two chapters was limited to particular companies that are on the leading edge of change in their respective industries, the present chapter broadens the focus to include an entire industry, banking, which is undergoing rapid change due to the implementation of informatics. In addition to exploring similarities and differences in specific job effects between insurance and banking, this chapter reveals whether there are company-to-company differences of approach, for instance, which might lead to different employment effects or at least alter the time frame of their appearance.

Banking is one of Canada's most venerable industries. In 1979, the five major chartered banks jointly held some $197 billion in assets, and

Table 5.1
FEMALE EMPLOYMENT IN FINANCIAL INDUSTRIES, CANADA, 1975 AND 1980[a]

Job Category	Female Employment		Change from 1975−1980	Females/Total Employment (both sexes) in Job Category, 1980	Females in Job Category/ All Females in Finance, 1980
	1975	1980			
Clerical	126,000	158,000	+32,000 (+25%)	90%	79%
Managerial and Professional	22,000	37,000	+15,000 (+68%)	35%	18%
All Job Categories[b]	153,000	201,000	+48,000 (+31%)	65%	100%

Note: a. June 1975 and June 1980.
    b. Includes job categories not shown above.
Source: From unpublished data supplied by the Labour Force Survey Division (Statistics Canada, 1980a).

contributed $2.3 billion to the gross domestic product (Statistics Canada, 1980*e*). Like the insurance companies, Canada's banks have been a major employer of women over the past twenty years. Not only has women's employment in banking increased by over 300 per cent, but their share of total employment in the industry has also increased to the point where it now approaches 70 per cent of total banking employment (Statistics Canada, 1980*a*).

As Table 5.1 demonstrates, women are fast increasing their representation in banks' sales and management ranks. But they are still heavily concentrated in the clerical ranks, with 80 per cent of female bank workers now in clerical positions.

THE TECHNOLOGY

While most of the basic informatics technology used in banking will be familiar by now, some of the combinations and features specific to banking deserve a separate introduction.

Automated teller machines (ATM), also called automated banking machines, are mature versions of equipment that was originally introduced a few years ago as cash dispensers. These machines feature a keyboard and an on-line link with the bank's computer facility. Programmed to handle a variety of transactions, such as deposits and withdrawals, the automated teller machines take banking a giant step toward becoming a self-service activity.

Personal access cards are the keys that activate the automated teller machines. When combined with a security code (or personal identification number), the personal access card substitutes for a signature. The customer first inserts the card into the automated teller machine, and then punches in the security code to authorize a self-service transaction.

Electronic funds transfer systems (EFTS) are used to instantaneously debit one person's account and credit another's. The major difference between this and other forms of electronic message transmission is that the information being sent is a command that is automatically acted upon at its destination. The command may be, say, to deduct an amount of money from a bank customer's account to pay for groceries purchased at a supermarket. The message would be relayed from the supermarket's point-of-sale terminal to the bank's computer, which would immediately transfer the funds and then relay back a message to the supermarket confirming that the initial command had indeed been acted upon. Other examples of the use of electronic funds transfer systems in banking are for pay-roll credits to employee accounts, as well as for interest payments to depositors' accounts. (See Chapter Six for a description of the use of point-of-sale terminals in retail trade.)

THE PROCESS OF AUTOMATION

From the advent of data processing in the early 1960s, it took just over a decade for the first phase of automation to permeate through the entire Canadian banking industry. The diffusion of informatics in the banking industry followed much the same pattern as that described for the insurance company in Chapter Four. The first phase was strictly limited to speeding up data processing. This eliminated much of the tedium of sorting transactions, processing interest charges, updating bank balances, and filing financial data. It also helped stimulate a demand for augmented services such as more detailed financial analysis (with its attendant clerical work), and it created fresh sources of work, such as in data-base management.

In turn, the expertise and systems thus developed allowed the banks to expand their range of services—multi-branch banking and daily-interest savings accounts being two examples. These services, and the on-line computer-communications networks required to provide them, were available at over 90 per cent of Canada's major bank branches by 1980—less than a decade after they were first introduced. Building on the basic on-line tie-in between the branch terminals and the banks' central computer facilities, most of the large urban branches were also offering computerized services for loans, savings, and term deposits.

Having moved from back-office to head-office information processing, and then to on-line information processing at the branches, the banks are now introducing the fourth phase of automation: interactive, on-line information processing for self-service banking. A highly integrated form of informatics, this phase is bringing the bank customer into direct and immediate contact with the banks' computer-based information system, rendering the teller increasingly obsolete.

Instead of dealing with banks by way of tellers, customers will increasingly deal directly with an automated teller or banking machine. By the end of 1980, there were an estimated one hundred such machines across Canada. By 1982, that number could be up tenfold, to over one thousand units. By 1985, when installations are expected to start levelling off, according to industry officials, there could be as many automated teller machines as there are brick and mortar branches today—about seventy-five hundred. By then, though, the name and functions of these machines could have changed, to something resembling a multi-purpose facility for shopping, bill paying, and other financial transactions including purchasing insurance and taking out various types of loans.

Currently installed automated teller machines allow the customer, acting alone, to make deposits and withdrawals, transfer money to other accounts, pay credit-card accounts, and obtain cash advances, plus pay the kind of bills (such as utility bills) that banks normally handle. The banks point out that these are only part of the total range of services that they offer to their customers. Still, these services represent a substantial portion of banking business—95 per cent in one bank.

The spread of automated teller machines will, in turn, spark other developments. For instance, when the ATM-related personal access card becomes widely distributed, at least one bank plans on using it in its traditional banks as well. The card will be inserted (not necessarily by the teller) into the counter computer terminal before transaction instructions are keyed in. Deposit, withdrawal, and transfer slips would then become quaint options, and possibly separately priced.

Automated teller machines will also hasten the automation of loan transactions. Much of the loans-servicing clerical work has already been automated. Already, short-term credit is available by way of credit-card cash advances, which are carried out on a partially automated basis. The next step will resemble the automation of group-insurance underwriting—a development discussed in the preceding chapter. Loan applications falling within the boundaries of a set norm will be processed automatically, according to pre-programmed standards. The loans officer and associated clerical staff will have to handle only the difficult cases.

EMPLOYMENT EFFECTS

The labour effects of the *first phase* of informatics in banking seem to have been relatively straightforward. New specialist positions were created and clerical work was transformed. Bookkeepers, ledger keepers, and file clerks, for example, became key-punch operators, computer operators, and tape librarians. Indeed, the number of clerical workers seems actually to have increased during this period, reflecting both the continued need for manual methods of information manipulation (such as key-punching and other encoding) in preparation for electronic data processing, as well as the labour requirements of extra services made possible by the new technology.

As evidence, it should be noted that not only did bank employment increase a substantial 56 per cent during this phase (in the 1960s), but the proportion of female employment also rose by almost 10 per cent. Since 80 per cent of all female employment in banking is concentrated in the various clerical positions, the proportionately larger increase in female employment indicates that clerical employment increases exceeded overall employment increases.

The *second phase* of informatics had more complex employment effects. There was an increase in the number of clerical job functions, consistent with the expansion of banking services, but not seeming to match the increases in other, professional, job functions. For instance, daily-interest savings accounts added substantially to the work-load of accountants and computer specialists, but contributed relatively little to the work-load of clerks.

As well, with the automation of some clerical tasks, there was an overall reduction in the labour content of providing many bank services. The automated teller machines, which automate the core functions of what tellers do, are obvious examples here.

There was also a truncation of job functions associated with completing banking transactions and generally providing banking services. One illustration concerns the changes stemming from the on-line connection. This system not only saves the teller from the after-hours work of preparing daily transaction records for the data centre, but also allows her to enter the transaction details directly into the data centre's computer. The teller thereby absorbs the data-entry clerk's job function to fill out her spare time.

On balance, it is generally asserted that the number of new transactions the technology made possible exceeded the amount of labour per transaction the technology eliminated. In fact, the technology is indirectly credited with much of the employment growth the banks experienced in the 1970s. (Employment grew by 67 per cent to exceed 153,000 by 1979.) Informatics technology is said to have made possible the additional services on which this growth was based.

However, during the 1975−1980 period, clerical employment growth lagged behind overall bank employment growth, a complete reversal of the experience during the first phase of informatics in banking. This suggests that although new clerical jobs were in fact created with the overall expansion of bank services, the clerical labour component of banking services decreased more than these increases in services could compensate for. The example of tellers absorbing the work of data-entry clerks sheds light on these dynamics.

The new jobs that were created with the advent of data processing are now either being automated themselves or the work is being amalgamated into other job categories. One bank official estimates that even before the introduction of automated teller machines, informatics-powered rationalization had already reduced the work of a traditional bank teller by half. As discussed earlier, the introduction of computer terminals into bank branches allowed central record keeping to occur simultaneously with the teller's initial compilation of information for the actual banking transaction. Hence, the teller was saved the work of preparing information for transfer to the central data centre.

Instead of the teller staff being reduced, though, new work was added to the teller job description—explaining the intricacies of new bank services, for example. However, some of the tellers' ''new'' work was in fact ''old'' work that had simply been transferred from other personnel in the bank—for instance, foreign-exchange services—and some was recycled traditional bank clerical work. Tellers now enter deposits and other data directly into the computer at the branch terminal; this is work that formerly had been done by data-entry clerks at the bank's data centre, and that was originally done by ledger-keepers transcribing from the tellers' own records.

One bank reports that employment of key-punch operators, data encoders, and other junior clerical workers is declining, not only in relative terms but in actual numbers as well. This follows the pattern first noticed among ledger-keepers during the first and second phases of bank automation. The significant difference is that with the pattern now applying to all junior clerical workers, entry-level job requirements have been moved up to the next level—involving more complex information handling. The jobs of tellers, cheque handlers, and related supervisory personnel are affected.

These jobs have already been indirectly affected by informatics, and with the third and fourth phases that are now being implemented—such as more automated functions and bank services—these jobs will also be affected directly.

Automated teller machines will reduce the teller's role in bank-customer relations from a central to a supporting one. As mentioned earlier, the personal access card substitutes a magnetic strip or microchip plus security code for a signature. Hence, it eliminates the need for all the forms and form signing traditionally needed to satisfy the signature-as-identification requirement. A bank customer need only sign once—when opening an account and receiving the personal access card. Since automated teller machines offer the most often-used bank services on a self-service basis, and since the banks envisage customers using their personal access cards even in brick and mortar banks, the number of tellers employed might be cut back substantially once those cards gain widespread acceptance (Canadian Bankers' Association, 1980). If that should happen, the dire predictions of 30 per cent or more unemployment in financial institutions (Nora and Minc, 1978, 1980) may not be so widely off the mark after all.

It will not be possible to chart the demise of the teller, however, since the job title is already disappearing. With the ongoing rationalization of banking operations, many banks have amalgamated branch clerical occupations and created a new classification called "administrative support," with several levels of work complexity. Interestingly, the former teller's position in this new hierarchy varies from bank to bank. At one, for instance, the new job title used is "customer service representative." (At another, however, that title corresponds to the former "supervisor of ledgers and tellers," a much more senior position.)

The new job description includes resolving customer complaints, promoting and selling banking services and related counselling. Corresponding to this enrichment of the clerical occupation, bank in-house training has been stressing techniques of customer relations and salesmanship. With the core of the work changing from passive information handling associated with traditional clerical work to more active information marketing, for instance, the banks seem to be creating a more professional information worker.

There is no agreement on net employment effects, however. One bank official predicts that in the future, the prerequisites for entry-level bank work will include a university-level education. Others maintain that high-school graduation will continue to suffice, although they stress that good marks and communications skills will be essential.

About one thing there is absolutely no dispute: banks are no longer the haven for clerical-level workers that they used to be. Clerical employment, which traditionally has grown faster than overall bank employment, began for the first time to lag behind overall growth in finance industry employment during the 1975–1979 period, according to figures from the Labour Force Survey Division at Statistics Canada. Total employment over those four years increased by 34 per cent; employment in the managerial and professional ranks increased by 42 per cent; but clerical employment grew by only 25 per cent.

Furthermore, the banks' own records show that banking employment, which had been growing at a rate of roughly 5 per cent a year through the 1970s, has now virtually stagnated, and even dropped somewhat. There were 154,000 people employed by the chartered banks in May 1979, which is nearly double the employment level of 1969. In May 1980, however, there were only 152,500; in August 1980, there were 153,000 (Canadian Bankers' Association, 1980). Thus the strong growth trend of the past seems to have come suddenly to an abrupt halt.

Changes in the teller function are only one example of informatics transforming clerical operations in the banking industry. Another major effect has been the gradual reduction in cheque-handling work both through electronic funds transfer systems, and more directly, through cheque truncation. Existing forms of electronic funds transfer include the automated, insurance premium payment system described in the previous chapter, as well as the electronic ledger system being introduced in stock exchanges to replace the physical movement of paper securities and payments. Further applications include the integration of electronic funds transfer systems with electronic cash registers to create point-of-sale systems in supermarkets and department stores. (See Chapter Six for more about the use of informatics in retail trade.)

Cheque truncation involves stopping the actual transfer of a paper cheque at any point along its payment-conveying route. One bank is currently considering a charge that is half the regular fee per cheque for customers willing to forgo having their cancelled cheques sent back to them. This would bring about significant savings in cheque-handling clerical work.

It is not possible to specify the *net* employment effects of banking automation. The amalgamation of jobs and the rationalization of banking operations have blurred job distinctions, even the formerly clear distinction between clerical and professional banking work. In addition, the banks' increasing use of part-time workers, facilitated by informatics, also makes the evaluation more difficult. In the past, when daily transaction records had to be prepared for the data centre after normal banking hours, most tellers had to be full-time employees. With that part of the tellers' work now automated, one bank reported that between 12 and 15 per cent of its employees work part-time.

That proportion, however, could increase substantially. If banks were to transfer more of their branch tellers and clerical staff to the data centres to work as telephone back-up personnel for the automated teller machines, most of the new jobs would likely be on a shift basis, as is the norm with telephone operators. At least one bank is considering this option.

The implications of this centralization, standardization and, possibly, segregation of banking clerical work, both in terms of job mobility and the quality of working life, will be discussed in Chapter Seven.

Before going on to the last case study—an industry study of the prospects for informatics in retail trade—this discussion will briefly explore some interesting developments in office-related informatics in banking.

A NOTE ON WORD PROCESSING IN THE BANKS

While there are elements of word processing involved in much of the informatics innovations discussed so far in this chapter (for instance, the message automatically printed on the bottom of account holders' monthly chequing-account statements), there is an interesting distinction between the approach of different banks to the use of this technology. One bank is approaching the automation of their strictly office information work from the integrative *télématique* perspective, while another is following the so-called *privatique* approach. The latter approach involves decentralized self-contained units based on distributed power rather than, as in the *télématique* approach, a centralized computer and an electronic communications network or "highway." (See Chapter Two for a description of the two approaches, and Chapter Three for an example of the *télématique* approach to general office automation.)

Only the *privatique* case will be discussed here. In that bank, word- and text-processing equipment was acquired in the spirit of a separate venture in office automation. The first stand-alone units were acquired in 1976 by the bank's credit-card processing centre to handle high-volume customer correspondence. Such units were later introduced in the information systems and administrative services departments, in each case to facilitate a particular, discrete information function, not to integrate them.

However, the information work has been centralized within each of these departments. Word-processor operators are grouped together at centrally located work stations in each department, and the administrative service work is done partially by the professionals and management personnel themselves and partially by a few administrative assistants.

These innovations have been credited with reducing clerical labour intensity by roughly one third. However, the bank has not had to reduce its clerical staff as a result.

The next and last case study will examine supermarket automation—and associated increases in employee productivity.

Chapter Six

Case Study: Supermarkets

So far, this report has looked in a general way at information work in technologically advanced office environments, then more specifically at this type of work in the head office of a large corporation in the transportation and communications sector. Finally, trends in how information work is handled in the widespread operations of a major insurance company, and in the banking industry as a whole, were examined.

In the case study on banking, two innovations were seen as pivotal breakthroughs permitting a whole range of further informatics applications. These were the on-line computer-communications linkages, plus the personal access card. Together, these made possible the advent of automated teller machines, truncated cheque and other financial paper handling, and various electronic funds transfer systems.

This chapter examines the potential of electronic funds transfer systems in retail trade as well as the extent of their use in Canadian businesses. As in banking, the process of diffusion of this technology in retail trade involves a few critical developments. These in turn enable the implementation of further informatics innovations and the realization of still further efficiencies. While much of the work and equipment involved in retail trade is common throughout the industry, this chapter focuses only on supermarkets, which seem to be on the leading edge of informatics innovation in the retail trade industry in Canada. The observations are not intended to apply to, much less to predict, what form informatics may take in the other retail industries.

Food stores have fared badly over the latter half of the 1970s. After fairly steady growth rates during the 1960s and steady although lower growth rates to 1975, the industry then faltered and started slipping. Measured in terms of real domestic product, the industry's income dropped by nearly 2 per cent between 1977 and 1979 to $1.3 billion (Statistics Canada, 1979*d*). At the same time, though, employment has continued to grow at around 3 per cent a year (Statistics Canada, 1980*b*). By 1979, there were 121,000 food store employees, 44 per cent of them female and over 50 per cent of them employed by a handful of major supermarket and foodstore chains that dominate the Canadian retail food industry.

Given the rising employment, declining returns, and high overhead in the retail food industry, it would appear that cost efficiencies could be a strong factor pushing supermarket automation. Before getting into the possible gains and the related employment effects, an introductory word on the critical technological developments relevant to this industry is in order.

Just as there seems to be an image of a wholly integrated future form of informatics in banking, insurance, and office work, so there is one in supermarket automation as well. This would be an electronic funds transfer system integrated with an automated check-out and bagger. Some of the key pieces of equipment and critical stages of development are described below.

THE TECHNOLOGY

The electronic cash register can ring up sales 10 to 20 per cent faster than the mechanical cash register. In addition, even the most basic stand-alone unit, in conjunction with an optical scanner (described below), also can monitor sales volumes and provide a daily breakdown on business according to major commodity groupings. Many Canadian supermarkets have more sophisticated models. These are programmed to provide detailed inventory monitoring, as well as to log the speed and sales volume of individual cashiers, and print a friendly message at the bottom of the sales slip.

Some electronic cash registers are connected to a mini-computer in the store, which when appropriately programmed can take a reading (rather like a meter reading) off the cash registers at any time and then massage those data to yield critical insights for reducing inventory overhead, or for increasing labour productivity. In other cases, particularly in the large supermarket chains, the electronic cash registers are connected directly to the head office "mother" computer. In the case of at least one supermarket chain in Canada, the head office computer regularly draws in all the raw data from the cash registers in various stores for centralized processing and analysis.

The optical scanner, first field tested in Switzerland in 1971, works on the same principle used for reading the magnetic strip on personal access and related cards. In this case, a laser beam "reads" information contained in the industry-standard Universal Product Code (UPC) symbol. Scanners can be either hand-held "wands," built into a check-out counter top, or the most sophisticated, remote controlled scanners. Some devices will also read the bar codes developed by supermarkets themselves for those items (generally perishables), which do not have the Universal Product Code. At least one supermarket chain in Canada has successfully tested these additional codes.

It is estimated that 70 per cent of merchandise has to be successfully scannable before significant productivity gains can be realized. Above that minimum mark, however, productivity gains tend to be exponential.

The point-of-sale (POS) terminal is an essential element in the implementation of supermarket automation. A basic point-of-sale terminal consists of an electronic cash register and scanner unit. More sophisticated systems are connected to a computer facility either in-store or at a central office. The most elaborate systems include electronic funds transfer capability—activated by the customer's credit card or personal access card and security code number. In such systems, the merchandise can be paid for by an electronic transfer of funds, with no bills or coins changing hands and no time wasted in counting out change and verifying it. Essentially, the correct combination of card and code number authorizes the sending of an electronic demand note to the customer's bank account, from which the amount of the bill is transferred into the supermarket's account. Such systems are being field tested in the United States and Europe, and are in the final planning and negotiating stages in Canada.

The technology for an almost completely automated check-out counter is already available. It is presently in use on an experimental basis in the United States and is currently being introduced in Canada, where two supermarket chains are expected to launch field trials of point-of-sale terminal systems by 1981.

THE PROCESS OF AUTOMATION

Experience in the United States demonstrates how quickly the technology can be diffused once the groundwork is laid, as well as how wrong diffusion predictions can be. According to a 1979 report (cited in *Canadian Grocer*, 1980), 953 United States supermarkets had scanner devices, almost double the 1978 total and over four times that of 1977. However, the number of installations fell far short of the figure of 7,800 projected for 1980 by a 1975 study (cited by Gilchrist and Shenkin, 1979). The 953 stores also represent a mere fraction of the 22,700 United States supermarkets in the over-$2 million annual sales bracket—a turnover considered the minimum to justify scanner installations.

Still, the speed at which the process of automation is taking place and the diversity of derivatory benefits are significant. The Giant Food Corporation pioneered supermarket automation with its first scanner-equipped check-out stand opened in 1973. By 1979, new installations were estimated (for all United States food stores) at 100 a month, depending on the availability of equipment. Further, virtually all new stores constructed in the United States were being equipped with electronic cash registers, and 65 per cent were on-line with at least an in-store computer (MacFarlane, 1980). This means that to complete the check-out automation process, scanner installations will be a relatively simple addition. Not only the ground work but the infrastructure will have been laid.

Adding to the cost-benefit incentive, a recent survey of scanner-equipped stores by the Food Marketing Institute (1980) found that nearly all of them are making good use of the data collected in the electronic cash registers. Using special software programmes for analysing the data, the stores glean information on the effectiveness of coupon and other promotions. They also gain cost-saving insights for work scheduling, shelf allocation, and inventory requirements. One nugget of market feedback was that merchandise displayed at adult eye level does *not* sell as fast as merchandise displayed one shelf down—opposite the eyes and grasping arms of the child seated in the shopping cart. The latest, and somewhat more moderate, prediction (Gilchist and Shenkin, 1979) for the diffusion of automated check-out systems in the United States calls for a 50 per cent penetration by 1984 and market saturation by 1988.

In Canada, no supermarket chain has scanners in more than 10 per cent of its stores, although two chains are expected to make major installations in 1981. Beneath this relatively calm surface, though, much has changed. Forms and management procedures have been standardized—a necessary precondition for maximizing the potential of the electronic cash register. As well, the requirements of metric conversion resulted in a massive change-over to electronic cash registers as well as weigh scales.

The industry is rife with ideas close to the launching stage, including plans for large-scale scanner conversions, as well as for point-of-sale electronic funds transfer systems for grocery-store payments. Major movements in these directions are felt to be imminent.

EMPLOYMENT EFFECTS

Even now, the preliminary steps already taken toward supermarket automation are affecting employment levels. For instance, the standardization of pricing sheets and inventory-and-reorder forms has allowed for a rationalization of store administration and reduced hours of labour required as a result. Similarly, the electronic cash register has helped increase efficiency by, for instance, tighter inventory control derived from the monitoring function of the cash register. Also, while there are no studies on productivity gains due to the computer monitoring of cashier performance, informal evidence suggests that there is a correlation. Cashiers say that having a computer print-out of daily keystrokes does exert a pressure to produce more. Adding to the pressure, they say, is that colleagues who fail to meet the store standard find their work hours reduced. (Some 60 per cent of supermarket cashiers work part-time.)

The United Food and Commercial Workers Union (UFCW), which represents a sizable proportion of supermarket workers in Canada, reports that since the mid-1970s, there has been a significant drop in the amount of overtime worked. There has also been a levelling off in the rate of hirings.

This suggests that a new labour situation—characterized more by a failure to replace or recall existing personnel than by massive lay-offs or firings, and by stagnation or jobless growth rather than absolute decline—may already be emerging in the retail food industry, even before wholesale conversion to scanner installations launches the industry into the next phase of supermarket automation. Subtly, at times almost invisibly, these effects must inevitably aggravate the overall unemployment problem, particularly in so far as women's work is concerned.

However, given their poor returns over the past three years, the Canadian food industry might not be financially prepared to invest great sums of money in scanners. As well, rising energy prices plus global crop failures threaten to force store owners to narrow their profit margins even as food prices rise to new heights; this too would tend to retard major capital investments in scanners. On the other hand, if the feedback from the United States experience is quite positive, this could provide the push needed to overcome the inertia of the negative factors just mentioned.

In Washington, D.C., Giant Food has recently moved ahead of Safeway as the area's leading supermarket chain. As of August 1979, Giant controlled 31 per cent of the market compared to Safeway's 25 per cent. Automation throughout Giant's stores was credited with the change: the automated stores were found to be drawing business from a wider area (Knight, 1979).

Interestingly, a Columbia University study (Gilchrist and Shenkin, 1979) exploring the effects of supermarket automation on employment isolated market expansion as the critical factor. The study suggested that the productivity gains made possible by scanner-equipped check-outs would enable stores having them to draw business away from neighbouring stores not similarly equipped. Hence, it argued, the major employment effects might be indirect, through job losses in other stores, rather than by direct loss in the store being automated.

This sheds light on the discrepancy between the potential and realized labour savings identified by Giant Food (1978) in a study of scanner-equipped stores. That study catalogued the rather impressive productivity-related savings potential shown in Table 6.1. On totalling the savings in the actual store setting, however, the Giant study maintained that they only amounted to 114 person-hours a week, or the equivalent of three full-time employees, for a total labour saving of 4.5 per cent. One possible explanation

Table 6.1
PRODUCTIVITY-RELATED SAVINGS POSSIBLE AT PEAK DEMAND FOR SUPERMARKET AUTOMATION

Origin of Savings	Savings at Peak Demand
Increased checker and bagger productivity	37%
Easier register balancing	21%
Automatic weighing and pricing	21%
Reduced errors in price reading, etc.	14%
Other	8%

Source: From an internal report produced by the Giant Food Corporation (1978).

is that the full savings can only be realized during peak-use periods, not when the system is idle or working at only partial capacity. However, the greater productivity and faster check-out service possible during those peak periods helped to drain considerable business away from competing stores.

One of the largest scanner-equipped supermarkets in Canada—Loblaw's Superstore in Ottawa—features eighteen checkout stands and does twice the weekly business of traditional supermarkets. It is reported to be drawing business away from three other supermarkets in the vicinity. Although no studies have been done, these stores report that sales are down substantially. They have not laid off staff, although with the scheduling flexibility part-time staff provides, lay-offs are not the only means of reducing staff.

Thus, while supermarket automation has yet to be fully implemented in Canada, the evidence to date certainly points to reduced labour demand.

CONCLUSION

This ends the case studies. They have looked at employment in several job and industry areas where women are most heavily concentrated. All four case studies have found profound employment changes occurring. Informatics is creating new work and employment, but largely in the professional and technical ranks where men predominate and women are still a minority. The retail food industry is no different; specialists in computer analysis and engineers with computer aptitude are in demand as are marketing and other sales specialists.

In all four cases, informatics seems to be eroding employment in traditional clerical work. The office of the future is one where many of the traditional office routines are performed automatically using an electronic rather than a paper medium for communication. The insurance office of the future is one where insurance policies are maintained automatically, and also in an electronic rather than paper and manila file form. The bank of the future is one where the customers serve themselves, requiring personal interaction, not for routine clerical and information-handling functions but for professional help and guidance. And the supermarket of the future is one where clerical information work will be incorporated into electronic machines for increasingly automated check-out as well as inventory control and pricing.

The next chapter will analyse the dynamics of change involved in this transformation process. It will also explore the possible overall effects of the changes identified in the case studies. Although these particular case studies cover only a small fraction of overall female clerical employment, the industries chosen and the jobs examined themselves constitute the majority of such employment. Therefore, it is not only possible to extrapolate from the particular to gain insights concerning the larger whole of women in the labour force, but it is necessary and important to do so in order to be able to formulate meaningful recommendations for possible preventive policy action.

Chapter Seven

Lessons from the Case Studies

The previous four chapters described how informatics technology is being introduced into several different Canadian industries. Chapter Three traced a company's transition into the "office of the future" from the cost-benefit-study stage through to 1980. Chapter Four looked at an insurance company with a relatively high level of informatics implementation and related organizational integration. Chapters Five and Six adopted an industry-wide perspective for discussing informatics in the finance industry and retail trade.

The present chapter summarizes the case-study observations, while the next chapter will explore the implications of those observations in four hypothetical scenarios.

PRODUCTIVITY

Perhaps the most significant of the research findings is that *the productivity of clerical workers is increasing*. Yet the effects of this rise in productivity are disguised by employment increases among other occupational groupings in the companies and industries affected.

The productivity gains are achieved in the following ways:

- By reduced labour content of clerical functions. This was apparent in everything from secretarial work to clerical work of all kinds in banking, insurance, and retail trade. With standardized paragraphs and a directory of names and addresses available in electronic storage, the secretary using a word-processing machine could have those paragraphs and addresses produced automatically, effectively substituting mechanical and electronic effort for her own.
- By fewer clerical functions for each type of service provided. This was graphically illustrated in the automated billing and premium collection used by the insurance company—the former clerical functions were all but eliminated.
- Through a truncation of clerical functions and the complementary amalgamations of formerly distinct clerical jobs. The banks offered an excellent example of this. With the teller now keying customers' transaction information directly into the bank's central computer, she not

only saves herself a lot of paperwork, but also bypasses certain clerical functions in the data centre.

- Through a reduction in supervisory requirements. While the case studies provided no statistics, they clearly identified two functions of lower-level management that informatics is usurping: performance supervision—now done by computer monitoring—and staff training—now largely done by computer-aided instruction.

- Through a compounding overall reduction in the clerical-labour content of information-related work. The insurance company vividly illustrated this dynamic. As more departments and more levels of the company (such as branch and regional offices) were integrated into the company's computer-communications network, the information put into the system by a clerical worker in one locale became immediately available to an ever-larger number of professionals, at no extra clerical cost.

Related to these changes, it appears that productivity gains can be achieved much faster where a *télématique* approach to informatics is followed. As explained in Chapter Two, the *télématique* approach features multiple access to a common telecommunications network. Once this "electronic highway" has been established within a company or industry group, information-handling work functions can be amalgamated fairly rapidly. By contrast, the *privatique*-type cases of informatics application suggest a slower rate of productivity gain because different types of information remain distinct and the related jobs, separate. An example from the present study is the case of the bank discussed in Chapter Six, which kept word processing separate from data processing.

In the cases studied, it appears that the *télématique* approach is fulfilling the prophecies inherent in Canada's strong transportation and telecommunications tradition, and that such a pattern could indeed become the predominant form of informatics implementation in this country. This dominance is particularly evident where the department first created by computer technology—data processing (or in recent years, information systems or management information systems)—takes the lead in introducing further information-related technologies, such as word- and text-processing equipment, into the company.

In some cases, departments within a company vie with each other for the lead in introducing informatics through the corporation. This has resulted in the data-processing and related services pitting themselves against such strictly office departments as administrative services. While the eventual victor will depend on factors too diverse for speculation, it appears that the data-processing group is triumphing, particularly in companies where a lot of the information work can be reduced to numbers. Banks, insurance and real-estate companies are obvious examples.

Since the companies studied seem to be leading the way in informatics innovation, it is possible that the approach they tend to take—the *télématique* pattern with its seemingly rapid productivity and employment effects—could become the standard for Canadian industry.

Another related observation from the case studies is that corporations tend to view office automation as part of a larger transformation of their entire information-related work functions. The prevailing image seems to fit the "pipeline" metaphor for information flows, which one corporate official used to illustrate both the design of and reason for the increasing integration of decision making between the company's sales, production, and strictly office operations. In keeping with this integrative and rationalized perspective, decisions on office automation are increasingly being made by senior management, in accordance with a company-wide informatics-based master plan. Furthermore, this plan usually includes major organizational changes, which sometimes precede the introduction of the actual informatics equipment.

The corporations studied seem to be aware that their fulcrum of control is shifting from cash flows to information flows. However, this will not necessarily lead them into the "post-industrial" age as described by Daniel Bell and others. Such a transition would require what Bell (1973, p. 115) describes as a shift in the axial principle of society. Just as an axis is the line around which a body turns, the axial principle is the central concept around which a society organizes itself.[1]

In Bell's analysis (and that of Thomas Kuhn (1970) is not dissimilar), society must shift from an energy-related to an information-related axial principle, for knowledge, not material goods, is the "energizer" of the post-industrial economy. Yet, as Stephen Peitchinis found in his survey of technological change in Canadian industry (1978, p. 125) and as Gordon Thompson laments in *Memo from Mercury* (1979, p. 10), Canadian industry is applying informatics technology along the axial principles (such as cost cutting and "concentrated benefit"), which have characterized the industrial age. These principles are not only inappropriate for an information-based economy, Thompson argues, but also actually suppress its development and jeopardize its job- and wealth-creating potential.

This problem of the overall orientation of society (toward energy or information, toward cost cutting or wealth creating) in itself deserves further study, for its resolution might offer relief from the employment-related concerns raised in the case studies. These concerns fall into three categories: unemployment, job mobility, and the quality of working life.

UNEMPLOYMENT

It is commonly agreed that the first phase of informatics actually generated extra employment. It created new ranks of specialist information workers and transformed, rather than eliminated, clerical work related to the recording, processing, and storing of that information. In addition, it allowed greater volumes of information work to be done.

While the case studies suggest that the second and third phases of informatics are still creating more employment, they also demonstrate a growing mismatch between the training and skills of female job seekers and the types of information-related employment being created. The professional and technical ranks are growing, while the clerical ranks—starting at the lowest-skill level—are in relative decline.

The negative effects on clerical employment are being hidden beneath the growth occurring in professional job ranks. The negative effects are further observed by the subtle form that clerical unemployment is taking: that of reduced job openings and unfilled job vacancies. Company officials acknowledge that the high turnover rates among female clerical, sales, and service workers facilitate their job restructuring and consolidation efforts. Turnover rates among women in these occupational groupings are consistently high. In 1979, for example, 30 per cent of female clerical workers had been at the same job less than a year (Statistics Canada, 1980c, Table 25).[2]

In the corporate office cited in Chapter Three, overall employment remained stable while the clerical ranks shrank by half. Yet only one of the displaced clerical workers was promoted into the professional ranks, while the remaining 100 were transferred to fill clerical job openings in other departments. The company case study in Chapter Four confirmed what Statistics Canada figures are revealing for the insurance industry as a whole: *clerical employment is declining*, not only in relative terms but also in absolute numbers. Moreover, if the experience of the major insurance company in that case study is at all representative of the industry as a whole, then the option of lateral transfers may disappear rapidly as informatics innovations transform the industry.

For many economic and social reasons, part-time work has become increasingly important in this industrial transition period. It can be a means of rationalizing job functions whose labour content has declined, and also is a way to share diminishing employment. At one bank where job openings decreased from a growth rate of 5 per cent annually during the early part of the 1970s to less than 1 per cent annually by the end of the decade, part-time workers now account for between 12 and 15 per cent of the work-force. In the supermarkets discussed in Chapter Six, over 50 per cent of cashiers are part-time employees. Many work fewer than twenty hours a week.

Although the ''ripple'' effects on unemployment are not specifically studied in this research, they deserve at least to be noted as a priority for further study. As the chapter on retail trade suggested, a scanner-equipped supermarket can draw business away from nearby stores and jeopardize new store openings. Similarly, as the banks expand into the new market area of management information and other business services based on their informatics capacity, they could usurp employment from existing small businesses that now provide those services.

JOB MOBILITY

Given the well-publicized shortages of systems analysts, data processing and other informatics professionals, it might be more appropriate to describe the "unemployment" problem discussed above as a mobility problem. The case studies of a large corporate head office and of a major insurance carrier highlight it well. For instance, as clerical labour demand diminished in the first company case study, virtually none of the workers affected was transferred to the expanding professional ranks; they were given lateral transfers or demotions. The second company studied had only limited success in moving its redundant clerical workers into their growing professional ranks. Some of the failures were moved back to clerical positions; others were asked to leave.

Part of this is an attitude problem. A typical response of management to the suggestion that a secretary performing administrative functions be moved into the executive ranks might well be a remark to the effect that, "You can't make a doctor out of a nurse."

Such attitudes compound the basic problem of an ever-widening skills gap between clerical-type information work and professional- and technical-type information work. The insurance company case study illustrated this well. The company used a scale of skill points to designate a job's complexity. Although the average skill points of clerical work were seen to be increasing, this was due largely to a decline in employment at the lowest skill-point levels. Meanwhile, the skill levels demanded of professional workers in the company rose by 2 per cent during one six-month period alone. Furthermore, this increase was largely accounted for by external hirings to fill the high-skill demand; it was not due to an overall upgrading of the company's existing staff.

Corroborating this concern, employers surveyed in 1978 expected that 60 per cent of people affected by future technological change would require more technical knowledge as well as sharper technical skills (Peitchinis, 1978, p. 147).

As available jobs increasingly move beyond the skills reach of the average clerical worker, the skills barrier to occupational mobility will tend to aggravate the even more intractable problem of chronic unemployment if no changes elsewhere in the economy are assumed. If clerical workers are unable to move up the skills gradient as quickly as the skill demands of information work increase, they will simply be left behind—a neglected human resource—when the informatics diffusion process reaches the point where lateral transfers to other clerical work become less of an option or possibly no option at all.

Besides the skills barrier, there are structural barriers to women trying to mobilize themselves out of clerical job ghettos. As the bank case study demonstrated, most women are concentrated in one area, with few access points that would allow them at least a chance for upward mobility. Further, the scope for mobility will decrease as companies capitalize on their informatics capacity in order to increase their output without increasing their employment. Jobless growth (employment stagnation associated with increasing output) is already evident in the transportation and communications segment of the service sector. Its share of Canada's real domestic product increased from 8.4 per cent in the 1960s to 9.4 per cent during the 1970s, yet its share of employment declined from 7.9 to 7.6 per cent.

The physical segregation of clerical work represents another structural barrier to mobility. As typists are moved into centralized word-processing work stations, their exposure to other work opportunities is effectively cut off. As one executive interviewed in the course of these case studies put it, "They (the word-processor operators) don't even know who we are."

Similarly, if bank tellers are moved into the banks' data centres to work as telephone back-up to the automated teller machines, their scope for advancement could also become more limited. Part-time work represents another somewhat similar mobility barrier. There seems to be an attitude of indifference toward the part-time worker, which is fortified by the negligible investment (in benefits, training, and so forth) that companies are willing to make in such workers. Yet part-time employment is a growing phenomenon among clerical workers and, increasingly, a work option women accept either because they have no other choice or because it fits their life-style more appropriately.

QUALITY OF WORKING LIFE

While this study has so far focused on the quantity of work being affected by informatics, the effects on the quality of work and working deserve some comment and concern as well.

The continuing standardization, streamlining, and fragmentation of work functions, which was observed in all of the case studies, suggests that clerical work is becoming more like an assembly line. The monitoring feature is also symptomatic: it tends to place quantity of output over sophistication of input, and thereby subtly degrades the scope of the work involved. Word-processor operators trying to demonstrate their knowledge of the firm, and thus their promotion potential, would be hard pressed to do so solely on the basis of their word-processing output.

Besides, the operation of a word-processor terminal does not require a great deal of skill on the part of the operator. The skills of good layout, formerly acquired over long experience, are all in the machine. As a word-processor work-station supervisor in Britain noted (cited by Barker and Downing, 1978), "A less experienced typist is able to produce the same quality of work as a really skilled girl and almost as quickly."

Some jobs are being enriched and thereby removed from the clerical category.[3] Many others, though, seem to be diminishing both in terms of the skill range required, and in terms of the scope for initiative possible.[4] The computer's silent monitoring of every action and its implicit pressure for greater output further depersonalizes the work-place. Women interviewed for this study complained that having a daily record of their number of keystrokes per hour (in data-entry work) or sales volumes (in cashier work), plus a detailed breakdown of their time away from the machine, acted as a source of anxiety to them.

Such effects could eventually produce the kind of social problems associated with assembly-line work. As well, by its implied stress on quantity, monitoring could also jeopardize the workers' chances for upward mobility, as its emphasis tends to frustrate efforts to do anything beyond rote clerical work.

In sum, then, the case studies indicate a radical upgrading of information work in Canadian industry, characterized by a diminishing demand for low-level clerical workers, an increasing demand for technical and professional workers, and a growing skills, educational, and aptitude disparity between the two occupational levels.

The next chapter will use scenarios to examine the possible future employment effects that may follow upon a more widespread diffusion of the same sort of informatics technologies examined in the case studies.

NOTES

[1] For example, de Tocqueville (1900) explained the spread of democratic feeling in American society in terms of the axial principle of equality.

[2] In 1975, 32 per cent of female clerical workers had been in the same job less than a year (Statistics Canada, 1980*a*). Labour force survey data on job tenure by occupation and sex are not available prior to 1975. A study by Price (1978), however, showed that female clerical workers employed by Air Canada, Ontario Hydro, and the Canadian Armed Forces in 1972 and 1973 had an average job duration that was less than half that of technical workers in the same organizations.

[3] This is so, for example, in the case of former secretaries who become administrative assistants, as described in Chapter Three. In other cases, such as that of bank tellers who take on greater marketing responsibilities, as described in Chapter Five, jobs may be enriched while retaining a predominantly clerical character.

[4] Secretaries who become power typists rather than administrative assistants, as well as some categories of telephone operators, are examples.

Chapter Eight

Scenarios For The Future

Numerous reasons to be concerned about possible diminished employment opportunities, barriers to job mobility, and lower quality of working life have been demonstrated. However, these concerns need a frame of reference for judging whether they are imminent or remote, real or academic, and without which it is difficult to stir policy makers to action.

For the policy maker who cannot wait patiently for the universe to unfold, but who must anticipate developments even before they fully emerge, the use of scenarios can help to provide at least a make-shift frame of reference. Since the scenario is merely a tool to aid thinking about the future, rather than a prediction or forecast, its content must be treated with extreme caution. However, by demonstrating the probable outcome of a certain combination of trends and assumptions, the scenario helps to point out the implications of that situation. It also allows steps to be considered and taken to initiate concrete policy actions intended to prevent undesirable situations from occurring, and to make desirable outcomes more likely.

Therefore, despite the small sampling of female clerical employment represented in the cases studied, despite the unknowns affecting the diffusion rate of informatics technology, and despite the possibility that the companies currently on the leading edge of informatics innovation might prove to be atypical in their approach and employment effects, some scenarios will be attempted.

The four case studies have shown that there is ample reason to fear that informatics could contribute to severe job displacement and reduced employment prospects among female clerical workers. On the one hand, the labour-reducing effects of informatics seem to have become concentrated in the clerical component of information-related occupations. As well, the implementation of informatics is widening the skills disparity between clerical and professional information-related work. Yet clerical workers generally have the fewest opportunities for educational leave and staff training, and women have particular problems upgrading their qualifications because of family and related considerations. In addition, women's recent penetration into traditionally male occupational preserves is relatively minor compared to their continuing strong concentration in clerical-type occupations. Hence, more and more young women entering the labour market and older women returning to it could become structurally unemployed, and risk long periods without work.

The scenarios will shed light on the possibility of structural unemployment by exploring the effect of different productivity gains and technology diffusion rates on clerical labour demand within the service sector. The results will then be compared to estimates of female clerical labour supply to the year 2000, based on the projected female labour-force participation rates discussed in Chapter One.

By focusing specifically on productivity-related employment shifts among clerical workers, the scenarios will attempt to demonstrate or refute the potential magnitude of this structural unemployment phenomenon. This in turn will illustrate the relevance, nature, and urgency of adjustment measures that should be considered.

OUTPUT ASSUMPTIONS

In the interest of simplicity, all four scenarios will assume the following growth rates for clerical output: 3 per cent annually during the 1980s and 2.5 per cent annually during the 1990s.[1]

Since the output assumptions are identical in all the scenarios, the two critical variables determining employment levels are thus the size of eventual productivity gains and the rate at which the enabling technology diffuses.

PRODUCTIVITY ASSUMPTIONS

It is evident from the preceding discussions that productivity gains from informatics can vary substantially depending on the industry and the approach to automation taken. Industries with a high information content—such as finance, insurance, and real estate, plus the utilities and business services—offer obvious opportunities for high productivity gains through informatics. Realization of those gains, however, seems to depend heavily on the approach taken. For instance, where one bank introduced word processing as a separate operation unconnected to its ongoing automation of financial data, a relatively low productivity increase was observed. By contrast, the first two companies studied (in Chapters Three and Four) attained more significant productivity gains through their more sweeping and integrated approach to informatics.

With the *télématique* approach, the dynamics of reduced clerical work per job function (and so forth) are applied over a larger number of clerical jobs and functions during a rapid and wide-ranging rationalization. In the *privatique* approach, the scope for rationalization is more restricted, for instance, to individual corporate departments and offices.[2]

Some of the research findings suggest that a high productivity gain (up to 50 per cent over the diffusion period) is possible where the *télématique* approach is used. For instance, in a department where all the information work had been integrated into a single electronic network, the clerical component of that department declined by 33 per cent over seven years. It was also estimated that traditional clerical-type office work could be reduced by 50 per cent through informatics. Therefore, 50 per cent will be used as the "high" productivity gain variable in the scenarios.

In the absence of specific productivity data for the *privatique* approach in the case studies, the scenarios will use as the "low" productivity increase the 33 per cent figure that has been cited in the literature on office automation and word processing (WPI, 1977).[3]

DIFFUSION ASSUMPTIONS

As discussed in Chapter Two, the diffusion rate assumption in the informatics-and-employment equation is subject to conjecture and to numerous countervailing factors. It is assumed here, however, that the factors tending to accelerate the diffusion process will outweigh possible restraining factors. It is also assumed that with the infrastructure for informatics largely in place, and the basic equipment relatively inexpensive and easy to use, the diffusion process could be more rapid than that observed for any previous technology.

The diffusion time will depend as much on how the technology is being applied as on its cost and availability, as well as on industry's understanding of how to exploit it. It appears that the diffusion process will initially proceed fairly slowly where companies are applying the technology according to a master plan of overall change and using the *télématique* approach; yet once the basic organization and structure are in place, additional purchases of informatics components can occur quite rapidly, with the possibility of making exponential productivity gains acting as a catalyst. The diffusion rate suggested under the *privatique* approach is somewhat steadier, starting off faster than, but never reaching, the maximum rate envisaged under the *télématique* approach.

The scenarios will explore two diffusion times: fifteen years (fast), and twenty years (slow). These two diffusion times will be used in combination with the two productivity-gain assumptions to produce four informatics scenarios.[4]

METHODOLOGY

Table 8.1 summarizes the output, productivity, and diffusion assumptions discussed above for each of the four scenarios. By dividing each year's output by the corresponding productivity level, an indication of the relative size of the work-force required is obtained, and these figures are also shown in the table.[5]

Multiplying the relative size of the work-force required by the absolute number of workers in the base year yields the total number of workers needed

Table 8.1
OUTPUT AND PRODUCTIVITY OF CLERICAL WORK, AND RELATIVE SIZE OF CLERICAL WORK-FORCE REQUIRED IN EACH OF FOUR INFORMATICS SCENARIOS, 1980−2000
(1980 = 100)

Year	Output All Scenarios	Productivity				Work-force Required			
		Scen. 1	Scen. 2	Scen. 3	Scen. 4	Scen. 1	Scen. 2	Scen. 3	Scen. 4
1980	100	100	100	100	100	100	100	100	100
1985	116	108	111	113	117	107	104	103	99
1990	134	117	122	125	133	115	110	108	101
1995	152	125	133	138	150	122	114	111	101
2000	172	133	133	150	150	129	129	115	115

Note: Scenario 1 assumes slow diffusion (20 years) and low productivity gain (33%).
Scenario 2 assumes fast diffusion (15 years) and low productivity gain (33%).
Scenario 3 assumes slow diffusion (20 years) and high productivity gain (50%).
Scenario 4 assumes fast diffusion (15 years) and high productivity gain (50%).

to produce the projected output—under the productivity and diffusion assumptions of each scenario. It is assumed that the proportion of females to total clerical workers will remain stable at its historic level of 80 per cent, so multiplying the relative-size-of-work-force figures by 1.4 million (the number of employed female clerical workers in 1980) gives the number of female clerical workers required in each scenario. This is the projected female clerical labour demand.

The next step estimates the size of the female clerical labour supply that would be available to the year 2000 under stated assumptions. These figures (shown in Table 8.3) are derived from the overall female labour-force participation projections discussed in Chapter One, by assuming simply that the proportion of women seeking clerical employment will remain at roughly a third of the female work-force. It should be emphasized that this assumption is *not* a prediction, but merely a means of demonstrating the possible effects of permitting that condition to remain unchanged.[6] It should also be noted that although the projections are carried out to the year 2000, only the first ten years are considered relevant from a policy perspective, given the uncertainty of most of the underlying assumptions.

In the last step, the projected labour demand figures are compared to the labour supply estimates. As shown in Figure 8.1, the results are, briefly, that the supply of clerical labour is projected to outstrip demand under all of the output, productivity, and labour-force participation assumptions considered. The extent and timing of the mismatch, however, depends on the particular combination of assumptions considered. The various possible combinations of variables will be examined in more detail in the following section.

In summary, then, the scenarios assume a growth rate for the service (or tertiary) sector of 3 per cent a year through the 1980s, and 2.5 per cent a year

Figure 8.1
INCREASE IN FEMALE CLERICAL EMPLOYMENT, CANADA, 1961−1979, WITH PROJECTIONS OF FEMALE CLERICAL LABOUR SUPPLY AND DEMAND, CANADA, 1980−2000

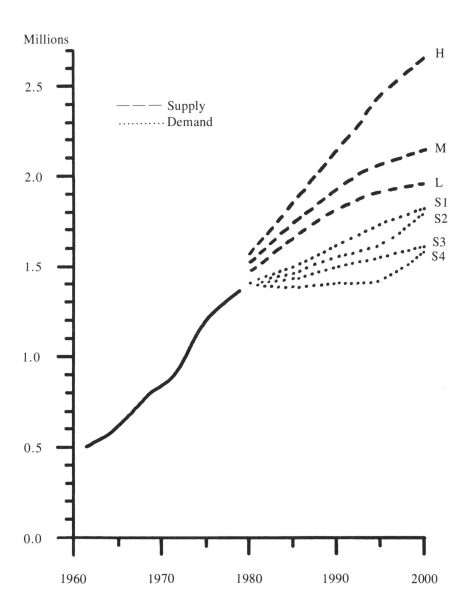

Table 8.2

NUMBER OF FEMALE CLERICAL WORKERS REQUIRED IN EACH OF THE FOUR INFORMATICS SCENARIOS, CANADA, 1980−2000
(in thousands)

Year	Scenario 1	Scenario 2	Scenario 3	Scenario 4
1980	1400	1400	1400	1400
1985	1500	1460	1440	1390
1990	1620	1540	1510	1410
1995	1710	1600	1550	1420
2000	1810	1810	1610	1610

Note: Assuming women continue to occupy 80 per cent of all clerical positions. Scenario output and productivity assumptions as in Table 8.1.

Table 8.3

NUMBER OF FEMALES SEEKING CLERICAL EMPLOYMENT, BASED ON THREE PROJECTIONS OF FEMALE LABOUR-FORCE PARTICIPATION, AND ONE PROJECTION OF FEMALE WORKING-AGE POPULATION, CANADA, 1980−2000

Year	Population 15+ $(\times 1,000)$[a] All Projections	Participation Rate (%)			Number Seeking Clerical Employment $(\times 1,000)$[b]		
		Low	Medium	High	Low	Medium	High
1980	9,388	47.1	48.2	49.8	1,470	1,510	1,560
1985	10,081	49.5	52.0	55.6	1,660	1,750	1,870
1990	10,670	51.3	54.5	60.8	1,820	1,940	2,160
1995	11,232	50.8	55.1	64.3	1,900	2,060	2,410
2000	11,787	50.0	54.6	68.0	1,960	2,150	2,670

Note: a. Based on Statistics Canada Projection No. 2, which assumes low fertility (1.7) and medium net immigration (75,000).

b. Based on population and participation rates shown, assuming a constant one third of women in the labour force continue seeking clerical employment.

Source: Population figures from Statistics Canada (1979c). Labour force participation rates from Denton *et al.* (1979) for the low projection, Zsigmond (1979) for the medium, and Ciuriak and Sims (1980) for the high.

through the 1990s. They also assume, and this is critical, that an unchanged proportion of the female labour force—one third—will continue seeking clerical work throughout the projection period. The scenarios explore two major variables, assigning to each certain values that have been derived either from the findings of this study or from outside authorities. For the first variable, productivity, a value of 50 per cent is used for the "high" productivity gain value, while 33 per cent is used for the "low" productivity gain. For the second variable, diffusion time, twenty years is used for a "slow" diffusion period, while fifteen years is used for the "fast" one. The scenarios are intended to demonstrate the effects that the diffusion of informatics-related productivity gains could have on clerical employment levels, and to point out the serious consequences this could create in terms of unemployment, unless major changes in the pattern of female occupational orientations are brought about at the same time.

For each of the four following scenarios, the results in terms of unemployment under each of the three labour force assumptions are summarized in Table 8.4, while Figure 8.2 shows the projected unemployment consequences of each of the four scenarios under the medium labour-force participation assumption.

SCENARIO 1: SLOW DIFFUSION, LOW PRODUCTIVITY

The first scenario assumes slow diffusion of a low productivity gain. Female clerical unemployment was 7 per cent in 1979. Under the conditions of Scenario 1, even with essentially no increase in female labour-force participation (low assumption), female clerical unemployment would increase to 10 per cent in 1985 and 12 per cent in 1990. If female labour-force participation were to increase only 5 percentage points over the next ten years (medium assumption), female clerical unemployment would rise to 14 per cent in 1985, and to 17 per cent in 1990. Were the participation rate to increase 11 percentage points over the next ten years (high assumption), female clerical unemployment would reach 20 per cent in 1985 and 25 per cent by 1990.

SCENARIO 2: FAST DIFFUSION, LOW PRODUCTIVITY

The second scenario assumes rapid diffusion of a low productivity gain. Female clerical unemployment would rise to 12, 16, or 22 per cent in 1985, depending on whether female labour-force participation is low, medium, or high. By 1990, the unemployment figures would be 16, 20, or 29 per cent respectively, under the three participation assumptions.

Table 8.4
FEMALE CLERICAL UNEMPLOYMENT RATES (%) ACCORDING TO FOUR INFORMATICS SCENARIOS AND THREE PROJECTIONS OF FEMALE LABOUR-FORCE PARTICIPATION, CANADA, 1980–2000

Year	Scenario 1			Scenario 2			Scenario 3			Scenario 4		
	Low	Med.	High	Low	Med.	High	Low	Med.	High	Low	Med.	High
1980	5.0	7.2	10.2	5.0	7.2	10.2	5.0	7.2	10.2	5.0	7.2	10.2
1985	9.9	14.2	20.0	12.1	16.3	21.8	13.3	17.5	22.8	16.4	20.4	25.6
1990	11.5	16.7	25.3	15.5	20.4	28.7	17.5	22.3	30.4	22.5	27.0	34.6
1995	10.2	17.3	29.1	15.8	22.4	33.5	18.6	24.9	35.7	25.4	31.2	41.0
2000	7.8	15.6	32.2	7.8	15.6	32.2	18.2	25.2	39.9	18.3	25.2	39.9

Note: For scenario assumptions, see Table 8.1. For details of participation rate projections, see Table 8.3. Female clerical unemployment was 7 per cent in 1979.

Figure 8.2
**PROJECTED FEMALE CLERICAL UNEMPLOYMENT UNDER
FOUR INFORMATICS SCENARIOS, WITH MEDIUM FEMALE
LABOUR-FORCE PARTICIPATION, CANADA, 1980–2000**

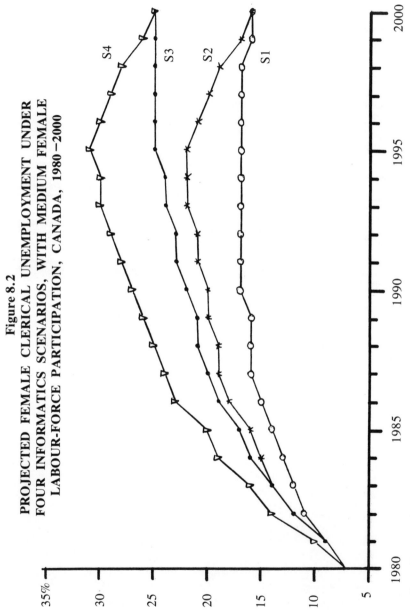

Note: For scenario assumptions, see Table 8.1. For participation rate projections, see Table 8.3.

SCENARIO 3: SLOW DIFFUSION, HIGH PRODUCTIVITY

The third scenario assumes slow diffusion of a high productivity gain. The results show an extension of the pattern produced by the previous scenario. Unemployment among female clerical workers is projected to rise to 13, 18, or 23 per cent in 1985, and to 18, 22, or 30 per cent in 1990, depending on the labour-force participation rate assumed.

SCENARIO 4: FAST DIFFUSION, HIGH PRODUCTIVITY

The fourth scenario assumes fast diffusion of a high productivity gain, and is the combination of variables that would have the most substantial effects on clerical employment. As the last column of Tables 8.1 and 8.2 indicate, this scenario projects an actual decline in clerical employment to 1985, and then virtual stagnation until 1990 or 1995. Even under the low labour-force participation assumption, female clerical unemployment would rise to 16 per cent in 1985 and to 23 per cent in 1990. Under the medium participation assumption, female clerical unemployment would rise to 20 and 27 per cent respectively, in 1985 and 1990. Under the high participation assumption, unemployment would attain 26 per cent in 1985, and 35 per cent in 1990.

DISCUSSION

All four scenarios suggest grim prospects for clerical workers in the years ahead. If the present pattern of training continues, with the present proportion of women seeking clerical employment, there will be a serious mismatch between skills and jobs. Even under the most benign of the scenarios and the most conservative of the labour-force projections, the unemployment rate among female clerical workers could attain 12 per cent by 1990—or nearly double the present rate of 7 per cent.

Under Scenario 4, with fast diffusion and high productivity, female clerical unemployment in 1985 could reach as high as 16 to 26 per cent (depending on whether female participation rates in the labour force are low or high), *if* the present proportion of working women continues to seek clerical employment. Under the same conditions, by 1990, the unemployment rate among female clerical workers could range from 25 to 41 per cent (under the low and high participation assumptions), assuming as before that approximately one third of working women continue seeking clerical employment.[7]

All of the scenarios set forth an alarmingly high rate of structural unemployment among female clerical workers, beginning as early as 1985, unless appropriate measures are taken by governments, employers, and women in the interim. Their message is clear. First, young women must be steered away from clerical-skill-level work because this line of work will not, in future, be able to absorb the high proportion of female workers who have, in recent years, been drawn to it. Second, many of the one and half million women currently engaged in such work must be helped to move into other lines of work before the diminishing job supply leaves them trapped by unemployment. Third, steps must be taken now before the skills gap between the work being automated and the work remaining grows too wide for even the most well-meaning employer and the most determined employee to bridge.

The concluding chapter will offer some suggestions for ameliorative policy action.

NOTES

[1] Obviously, if the level of output were assumed to be higher, the amount of work required to produce it would be greater; conversely, if the output level were lower, less labour input would be needed.

[2] As discussed earlier, the term *privatique* has been applied to the more isolated and discrete implementations of informatics, while the term *télématique* is applied to the more sweeping, all-encompassing approach. The productivity gains in each revolve around the scope for the rationalization of employment that each offers.

[3] If the productivity gain assumed were greater, less labour input would be required to produce the same output, but if the productivity gain were smaller, more workers would be needed.

[4] Faster diffusion would cause an earlier appearance of the employment effects of the technology, while slower diffusion would delay the appearance of those effects.

[5] The translation of productivity levels into work-force size assumes that there will be no change in the number of hours of work per year per employee. Fewer hours, which are probable the longer our time horizon is, would mean that the same amount of work would require a larger work-force.

[6] The longer the time horizon considered, the less likely this static assumption is to remain valid. As was seen in Chapter One, the historic trend has been in the direction of an increasing proportion of women in clerical occupations. However, if the demand for clerical labour decreases as a result of productivity gains, the decreased demand would eventually be expected to lead to a contraction in the size of the clerical labour force. Nevertheless, in the face of continuing expansion of overall female labour-force participation, this would not necessarily lead to an improvement in the projected female unemployment problem, unless the employment outlook was substantially better (and of sufficient magnitude) in other occupations or industries.

[7] While such high levels of unemployment would undoubtedly produce negative feedback effects tending to reduce the number of women seeking clerical employment, serious damage might have already taken place by that time. In the past, educational institutions in particular have been slow to adjust to changed conditions. In the early 1970s, for example, even after the market for new teachers had shrunk to a fraction of its former size, teachers colleges and university departments of education continued for several years turning out large numbers of prospective teachers, in spite of the fact that the reduced demand for teachers was foreseen long in advance.

Conclusion

Summary and Recommendations

Canadian women are on a collision course between their continuing concentration in clerical occupations and industry's apparently diminishing requirements in that line of work. On the supply side, a high proportion of women are now dependent on clerical and related work as a mainstay in their increasingly long-term working lives. On the demand side, though, clerical employment is declining as informatics erodes the labour content of information-handling work.

This increasing divergence between, on the one hand, a growing supply of female clerical labour, and on the other, a rapidly collapsing clerical labour demand, could, unless appropriate measures are taken, lead to nearly a million women being without employment by 1990 if our assumptions are correct. The possibility of such structural unemployment could be reduced if the problem that presages it—lack of occupational mobility—is tackled aggressively in the 1980s. The informatics technology that is threatening to reduce clerical employment is also stimulating employment in an expanding range of new professional and technical information-related occupations. The new jobs, however, are more demanding, posing a potential mobility problem to those being displaced from or finding no job openings in clerical work. This problem could be overcome through programmes of high-technology training and affirmative action, in effect mobilizing women to benefit from the new technology.

Today, the problem is one of mobility. By 1990, the already widening skills disparity between clerical and professional information work may have grown to the point where displaced clerical workers might be unemployable without further training. The problem becomes all the more urgent given the particular nature of what we envisage as higher potential unemployment, which appears from our case studies to be assuming the form of reduced job openings and unfilled job vacancies. Neither form makes headlines, although the frustrated potential workers could eventually contribute to higher unemployment statistics, unless they get so discouraged as to not start looking for, or to give up looking for, work altogether.[1]

Another potentially serious feature of the problem is that with the heavy concentration of women in the occupations negatively affected by informatics, the reduction in job opportunities could come to be seen as a uniquely ''female'' problem, of only marginal importance to men, who predominate in the occupations being enriched and enlarged by informatics. Aggravating this concern, there appears to be a lingering but pervasive notion in our society that women are characteristically only a ''secondary'' part of the labour force, not as attached to working nor as important to the Canadian economy as are men (Economic Council of Canada, 1976).

Recent studies indicate, however, that 60 per cent of women work because they have to. They are either living alone, single parents, or married to someone who earns less than $10,000 a year. The *Women and Poverty Report* (National Council of Welfare, 1979), for example, pointed out that in nearly 50 per cent of the cases where both husband and wife work, their combined income is less than $15,000. It is further pointed out that if the wife were not working, the number of Canadian families living below the poverty line would increase by 50 per cent.

It is entirely possible that such a situation could in fact befall many Canadian families by 1990 if not before. According to the scenarios discussed in the previous chapter, female clerical workers could experience unemployment of the proportions currently being experienced by auto workers in central Canada. With existing informatics capable of automating information-handling work to the extent revealed in this report, and with informatics diffusing at a rate projected earlier in this report, by 1990 there could be work for only half to two thirds of the potential number of Canadian women who might be seeking employment as bank tellers, cashiers, and other clerical positions in industry and government.

Governments must recognize the urgency of encouraging young women to look elsewhere for jobs rather than to traditional clerical work. They must also work to stimulate occupational mobility to prevent a situation in which severe structural unemployment in the 1990s could disrupt Canada's social and economic stability.

In terms of concrete action, the following broad governmental initiatives are suggested.

An information and education campaign should be launched by the federal and provincial governments to help alert women to what informatics is doing to traditional clerical work, and to encourage industry to draft specific job-mobility programmes for their clerical employees. It could be argued that such programmes would be as much in industry's self-interest as in the interests of women and of stable employment. Unless women are trained for the emergent information professions, Canada could face a severe labour shortage in these skill areas, which in turn could jeopardize Canadian information industries and the success of Canada's transition to the post-industrial era.

Existing manpower training and counselling programmes for women should be retailored so as to emphasize jobs having a better long-term outlook. Also, alternative training options—such as on-the-job educational partnerships between government and industry—should be explored.

A special tri-partite (industry, labour, and government) task force on employment adjustment and informatics should be created. The task force would undertake further research into this critical area of technological change. Among its responsibilities, the task force should address itself to the general questions raised regarding Canada's transition into the post-industrial age—including such regional dimensions as Alberta's emergence as a major economic force.

The proposed task force should also examine such specific questions as the possibility that as informatics becomes more widespread, there could be fewer jobs available than people wanting to work. Enlarging the scope of relocation aid to cover clerical as well as professional workers would be one obvious solution. Eventually, however, more imaginative strategies will be required.

All segments of Canadian industry except for public administration are showing a declining labour intensity (Economic Council of Canada, 1980). The service sector, which has been such a bountiful supplier of new employment opportunities over the last twenty years, seems to be reaching a plateau in terms of employment. In fact, with informatics eroding its clerical labour component and intensifying employment at the more senior levels, the entire sector could be entering a state of relatively static employment, although there are indications that the demand for domestic services will continue to increase.

The task force should also explore means of sharing the available job opportunities. Paid educational leave, a shorter work week, part-time working arrangements, and more statutory holidays are among the many mechanisms that could be studied for their feasibility.

More specific recommendations follow, related to education, job counselling, employment security, additional research needed, and statistical data requirements.

Perhaps the major point to emerge in the Organisation for Economic Co-operation and Development (1976) report on Canada's educational system is that our education policy needs to be more closely integrated with national policies and economic realities. According to the study, Canada gets high marks for education as an end in itself, but low marks for education as a means to economic ends.

Governments should launch a major computer-education campaign to drastically increase the computer literacy of Canadians. The Japanese example in this respect may be worth studying. That country is in the midst of a campaign aimed at increasing the computer-educated population in Japan from 3.5 million in 1975 to 15.5 million by 1985. Including adults as well as students at schools, colleges, and universities, such a campaign could help to close the gap between what goes on in educational institutions and what goes on in the economy.

Far from helping women overcome barriers to occupational mobility, there is some evidence that *government manpower training programmes for women have actually heightened the barriers and made occupational segregation more rigid.* A recent study (Dale, 1980) of government employment strategies for women, for example, revealed that over half the female trainees in occupational skill-training programmes are being taught clerical skills. Even in apprenticeship training, most of the women are concentrated in traditionally female personal services—such as cooking and hairdressing. Therefore, *government manpower training programmes for women must be reoriented toward informatics and other microelectronic technologies that are stimulating new areas of industrial activity and employment.*[2] Further, since the scope of upgrading requirements is getting larger, the training programmes must themselves be enlarged to cover as wide an area as possible.

Both the federal and provincial governments should develop joint government-industry education-apprenticeship programmes that would combine technical education with skills training. The University of Waterloo's co-operative programme could be taken as a model; students alternate between the campus and industry throughout their studies. Furthermore, such programmes should become part of an overall career strategy in which education is a continuing feature in a person's working lifetime, rather than a one-shot preparation for the work-force with perhaps an occasional stint of upgrading study.

The proposed task force on employment adjustment and informatics could undertake this strategy-cultivation work. In so doing, it should be guided by the recommendations contained in a report on educational leave and working Canadians recently published by Labour Canada (Adams, 1979). In particular, it could immediately move to *study the feasibility of creating a registered educational leave plan.* Drafted on the lines of the successful Registered Retirement Savings Plan (RRSP), this plan would provide a specific mechanism by which to achieve the education-work policy. It would allow those who could afford to save for their own educational upgrading to do so at a tax advantage. The use of refundable tax credits rather than tax deductions, with or without bursaries, would help make educational leave available to all income groups on a more equitable basis.

The Government of Canada (and provincial governments as well) should establish target figures for pay-roll expenditures on personnel education and training, applicable both to industry and to itself. Given the major increase in education envisaged by the preceding recommendations, the 2.2 per cent of pay-roll that the federal government currently devotes to personnel training is clearly inadequate.

In addition to the skills and educational barriers, women also face structural barriers to occupational mobility. As has been documented in recent sociological research (Rosenfeld, 1979; Boyd and Humphreys, 1979), women often have fewer opportunities for advancement simply because such opportunities are not a feature of the occupations in which they are concentrated. A secretary-typist often remains a secretary-typist all her working life. Similarly, telephone operators, bank tellers, and cashiers have relatively little scope for career advancement. In light of this, *training programmes should be supplemented with occupation-bridging mechanisms and affirmative-action programmes designed so that women can put their training to work.* To emphasize the importance of such mobility measures, and they are critical, governments should consider making such programmes mandatory for companies receiving government contracts.

COUNSELLING

Attention should be given to psychological and emotional barriers to women's occupational mobility. Therefore, *government employment strategies for women should provide for counselling concerned with change-promoting techniques.* In addition, *the government should set up a special grant programme to fund self-help endeavours—such as women's "networking" schemes—aimed at promoting occupational mobility by pooling contacts, experience, and moral support.*

EMPLOYMENT SECURITY

Women—particularly the clerical workers among them—are uniquely unprotected against the negative employment effects of informatics. On the basis of our evidence, unemployment in this sector seems to be an ever-present possibility. Further, women on the whole are an unorganized labour force. Even in the most unionized province, Ontario, fewer than 30 per cent of female workers are union members. Less than 1 per cent of bank workers are unionized. So, most women lack even the minimal protection offered under most union-contract technological-change clauses. In light of this situation, the government should introduce special measures to protect them against informatics' negative effects, as outlined below.

The Canada Labour Code should be amended to include the protective measures recommended by the Carrothers (1979) Commission of Inquiry into Redundancies and Lay-offs.

The federal government should consider introducing legislation establishing benefits for part-time workers within its jurisdiction comparable to those available under full-time employment.

ADDITIONAL RESEARCH NEEDED

A recent study by the Massachusetts Institute of Technology (cited in Lund, 1981) suggests that most new employment growth is occurring in firms with fewer than twenty employees. At the same time, it is the small-size firms that account for much of the explosive market growth for mini- and micro-computers. Therefore, *the governments of Canada should consider sponsoring some case-study research into the employment effects of informatics on small firms.*

The Social Sciences and Humanities Research Council is laying the groundwork for a pioneering programme of research and study called the Human Context of Science and Technology. Within this programme, strong consideration should be given to funding a conference in which academics and non-academics could discuss the employment implications of informatics on the female labour force, and to funding research that would explore the quantitative and qualitative employment effects of informatics implemented under a *privatique* versus a *télématique* approach.

It would also be worth studying the career attitudes of high-school students in a school equipped with computers and computer education aids, and comparing these with attitudes in a school without such facilities. Such a study could provide useful guidance in establishing a nation-wide computer-literacy campaign.

STATISTICAL DATA REQUIREMENTS

The job-vacancy survey ought to be revived. It would provide a much needed measure of cross-industry fluctuations in occupational employment. Without it, a researcher is left with labour-force statistics by occupation on the one hand and employment statistics by industry on the other. The two are irreconcilable.

The government should consider establishing labour-industry research advisory committees for each industrial sector, similar to those set up by the United States Bureau of Labor Statistics.

CONCLUSION

Canadian women are under serious threat because of their concentration in occupations that are being swept aside to make way for the new information society of the post-industrial era. They are further threatened because they lack the mobility—financially and educationally—to adapt to the changing labour demands. If they are not able to adapt, the unemployment they will suffer could have serious consequences both for them and for the national economy. If they are able to adapt, they could help to boost Canada into a buoyant post-industrial condition. The determination of which result is to ensue will depend on early and effective action by governments, employers, and women themselves.

NOTES

[1] In the latter case, they are no longer included in the official unemployment count.

[2] A list of occupations expected to be in future demand appears in the Appendix.

Appendix

Occupations With Good Future Prospects

Recent surveys of skill and occupational shortages in Canada suggest that the jobs of the future will increasingly require a degree of computer literacy as well as technical ability to operate computer systems and manipulate the associated software.

The most consistent demand will be for people capable of operating computer systems, at various levels of sophistication (Newton, 1980). Starting with the most skilled, these occupations would include electrical and electronic engineers, technologists, and technicians; systems analysts; senior analysts; senior programmers; technical programmers; systems programmers; data processors; data encoders.

There will also be a demand for specialists in graphics, telecommunications, hardware, training, and sales related to different informatics applications and computer- or microprocessor-based systems.

A detailed description of the activities and educational requirements associated with each occupation and job function is available in the publication, *Informatics*, prepared as part of the Occupational Analyses Series, Employment and Immigration Canada (Coopers, Currie and Lybrand Ltd., 1980).

A study of overall skill requirements in Canadian industry published recently by the Economic Council of Canada (Betcherman, 1980) predicts a growing problem of filling skilled blue-collar jobs, particularly in product fabricating and repair machining. It also identifies a skill-shortage problem in white-collar occupations, particularly engineering, engineering technicians, systems analysts, and managerial personnel in financial institutions.

References and Bibliography

Adams, R.J. 1979. *Education and Working Canadians*. Report of the Commission of Inquiry on Educational Leave and Productivity. Ottawa: Minister of Supply and Services Canada.

Barker, Jane and Downing, Hazel. 1978. *Word Processing and the Transformation of Patriarchal Relations of Control in the Office*. Discussion paper for the CSE Microelectronics Group. Dagenham, Essex: N.E. London Polytechnic, Centre for Alternative Industrial and Technological Systems.

Barron, Iann and Curnow, Ray. 1979. *The Future with Microelectronics: Forecasting the Effects of Information Technology*. London: Frances Pinter.

Bell, Daniel. 1973. *The Coming of the Post-Industrial Society: A Venture in Social Forecasting*. New York: Basic Books.

Bergom-Larsson, M. 1979. *Women and Technology in Industrialized Countries*. Working Paper No. 8. New York: United Nations Institute for Training and Research.

Betcherman, Gordon. 1980. *Skills and Shortages: A Summary Guide to the Findings of the Human Resources Survey*. Research study. Ottawa: Economic Council of Canada.

Bossen, Marianne. 1976. *Employment in Chartered Banks 1969–1975*. "Sponsored by the Advisory Council on the Status of Women and the Canadian Bankers' Association." Winnipeg: M. Bossen and Associates.

Boyd, Monica and Humphreys, Elizabeth. 1979. *Labour Markets and Sex Differences in Canadian Incomes*. Discussion Paper No. 143. Ottawa: Economic Council of Canada.

Canadian Bankers' Association. 1980. Unpublished statistics communicated to the author. Toronto.

Canadian Grocer. 1980. "Scanning Units Installed in U.S. Soar to 953." *Canadian Grocer* (May).

Carrothers, A.W.R. 1979. *Report of the Commission of Inquiry Into Redundancies and Lay-offs*. Ottawa: Minister of Supply and Services Canada.

Chisholm, D.A. 1978. "Communications and Computers: Information and Canadian Society." A Position Paper. Ottawa: Science Council of Canada.

Cirrito, Marianne J.; Goshdigian, Florence K.; and Willson, Katherine H. 1980. *Forecasts Relevant to Office Productivity*. Scout Report (unpublished literature review) No. 478-106-05, prepared for the Futures Studies Program, Institute for Research on Public Policy, Montreal. Glastonbury, Connecticut: The Futures Group, Inc.

Ciuriak, Dan and Sims, Harvey. 1980. *Participation Rate and Labour Force Growth in Canada*. Papers on Medium and Long-Term Economic Issues. Ottawa: Department of Finance, Long Range and Structural Analysis Division.

Computer/Communications Secretariat. 1978. *The Growth of Computer/Communications in Canada*. Ottawa: Department of Communications, Computer/Communications Secretariat.

Coopers, Currie and Lybrand Ltd. 1980. *Informatics*, by R.J. Adams and M.R. Applin. Occupational Analysis Series. Ottawa: Employment and Immigration Canada, Occupational and Career Analysis and Development.

Dale, Patricia. 1980. *Women and Jobs: The Impact of Federal Government Employment Strategies on Women*. Ottawa: Canadian Advisory Council on the Status of Women.

Denton, F.T.; Feaver, C.H.; and Spencer, B.G. 1979. "The Future Population and Labour Force of Canada: Projections to the Year 2051." A Background Study for the Economic Council of Canada, as cited in Economic Council of Canada, *One in Three—Pensions for Canadians to 2030* (Ottawa: Minister of Supply and Services Canada, 1979).

Department of Labour, Women's Bureau. 1980*a*. *Women in the Labour Force 1977*. Ottawa: Minister of Supply and Services Canada.

Department of Labour, Women's Bureau. 1980*b*. *Women in the Labour Force 1978 – 1979*. Ottawa: Minister of Supply and Servies Canada.

De Tocqueville, Alexis, 1900. *Democracy in America*. New York: P.F. Collier.

Dominion Bureau of Statistics. 1967*a*. *The Demographic Background to Change in the Number and Composition of Female Wage-Earners in Canada, 1951 to 1961*. Cat. No. 71-511. Ottawa: Queen's Printer.

Dominion Bureau of Statistics. 1967*b*. *Seasonally Adjusted Labour Force Statistics: January 1953 – December 1966*. Cat. No. 71-201. Ottawa: Queen's Printer.

Economic Council of Canada. 1976. *People and Jobs: A Study of the Canadian Labour Market*. Ottawa: Information Canada.

Economic Council of Canada. 1980. Personal communication to the author based on an unpublished analysis of data from Statistics Canada.

Food Marketing Institute. 1980. Unpublished report cited in the *Canadian Grocer* (May 1980). Washington, D.C.

Freeman, C. 1977*a*. *The Kondratiev Long Waves, Technical Change and Unemployment*. "This paper has been reviewed and is being published by the OECD as part of the Conference Proceedings, Expert Meeting on Structural Determinants of Employment and Unemployment, 7 – 11 March 1977, Paris." Sussex, England: University of Sussex, Science Policy Research Unit (SPRU).

Freeman, C. 1977*b*. *Technical Change and Unemployment*. Paper presented at the conference on Science, Technology and Public Policy: An International Perspective, University of New South Wales, 1–2 December 1977; to be published in conference proceedings. Sussex, England: University of Sussex, Science Policy Research Unit (SPRU).

Ganley, Oswald H. 1979. *The Role of Communications and Information Resources in Canada*. Program on Information Resources Policy. Cambridge, Massachusetts: Harvard University and the Center for Information Policy Research.

Giant Food Inc. 1978. "Savings with the Computer-Assisted Check-Out at Giant." Internal report.

Gilchrist, Bruce and Shenkin, Arlaana. 1979. "The Impact of Scanners on Employment in Supermarkets." Progress report. New York: Columbia University, Department of Computer Science, July (revised December).

Goracz, A.; Lithwick, I.; and Stone, L. 1971. *The Urban Future*. Research Monograph No. 5. Ottawa: Central Mortgage and Housing Corporation.

Hough, R.W. and Associates Ltd. 1980. "Office Automation Equipment: The Present Base and Future Prospects to 1985." Draft report, edited by M. Estabrooks and L.A. Schakelton. Ottawa: Department of Communications, Communications Economics Branch.

Jackson, D.N. and Williams, D.R. 1974. "Influences Upon the Development of Vocational Interests." A Study by the Vocational Interest Research Unit. London, Ontario: University of Western Ontario, Department of Psychology.

Kettle, John. 1980. *The Big Generation*. Toronto: McClelland and Stewart.

Knight, Jerry. 1979. "Giant's Last Check-Out Computerized." *The Washington Post* (14 August), p. 9.

Kuhn, Thomas. 1970. "Structure of Scientific Revolutions." *International Encyclopedia of Unified Science*, Vol. 2, no. 2. Chicago: University of Chicago Press.

Kuyek, Joan Newman. 1979. *The Phone Book: Working at the Bell*. Kitchener: Between the Lines.

Lamberton, D. 1978. "Social Costs of Change, Employment, Professional Skills and Curricula." Discussion paper prepared for the OECD Working Party on Information, Computer and Communications Policy.

Lund, Robert T. 1981. "Microprocessors and Productivity: Cashing In Our Chips." *Technology Review* 83 (January): 32-44.

Lussato, Bruno and Bounine, Jean. 1979. *Télématique . . . ou Privatique? Questions à Simon Nora et Alain Minc*. Paris: Editions d'Informatique.

MacFarlane, Stephen J. 1980. "Computers in Retailing." *Canadian Datasystems* 12 (May): 29-37.

McLean, J. Michael. 1979. *The Impact of the Microelectronics Industry on the Structure of the Canadian Economy*. Occasional Paper No. 8. Montreal: The Institute for Research on Public Policy.

McLuhan, Marshall and Fiore, Quentin. 1967. *The Medium Is the Message*. New York: Random House.

McNair, Malcolm P. and May, Eleanor G. 1978. "The Next Revolution of the Retailing Wheel." *Harvard Business Review* 56 (September/October): 81-91.

National Council of Welfare. 1979. *Women and Poverty*. Louise Dulude, Project Consultant. Ottawa: National Council of Welfare.

Newton, Keith. 1980. "Forecasting Skill Shortages" Speech to the Canadian Manufacturers Association, May. (To be published as an article by Keith Newton, Gordon Betcherman, and Noah Meltz, "Diagnosing Labour Market Imbalances," *Canadian Public Policy*, forthcoming).

Nora, Simon and Minc, Alain. 1978. *L'Informatisation de la Société*. Paris: La Documentation Française.

Nora, Simon and Minc, Alain. 1980. *The Computerization of Society*. A translation of *L'Informatisation de la Société*. Cambridge, Massachusetts: MIT Press.

Organisation for Economic Co-operation and Development. 1976. *Reviews of National Policies for Education: Canada*. Paris: OECD.

Organisation for Economic Co-operation and Development. 1980. *Reviews of National Policies for Education: Canada*. Paris: OECD.

Osborne, Adam. 1979. *Running Wild: The Next Industrial Revolution*. Berkeley. California: McGraw Hill.

Palmer, John L., ed. 1978. *Creating Jobs: Public Employment and Wage Subsidies*. Studies in Social Economics. Washington, D.C.: The Brookings Institution.

Peitchinis, Stephen G. 1977. *Technological Changes in Banking and the Effects on Employment*. Research Report, Technological Innovations Studies Program. Ottawa: Dept. of Industry, Trade and Commerce, Technology Branch.

Peitchinis, Stephen G. 1978. *The Effects of Technological Changes on Educational and Skill Requirements of Industry*. Research Report, Technological Innovations Study Program. Ottawa: Dept. of Industry, Trade and Commerce, Technology Branch.

Peitchinis, Stephen G. 1980. *Technological Changes and the Demand for Skilled Manpower in Canada*. Studies on the Employment Effects of Technology. Calgary, University of Calgary, Department of Economics.

Porter, M.R.; Porter, J.: and Blishen, B.R. 1979. *Does Money Matter?* Revised version of a 1978 study done for the Government of Ontario. Toronto: Macmillan.

Price, W.L. 1978. "Mesure des taux de roulement des travailleurs dans l'industrie canadienne." *L'Actualité économique* 3 (July-September): 402-9.

Robinson, Peter and Shackleton, L.A. 1979. *National Policies and the Development of Automatic Data Processing*. A synthesis of six country reports, prepared for the Data for Development Conference. Ottawa: Department of Communications, Telecommunications Economics Branch.

Rockman, Arnold. 1980. "Notes on the Coming of the Wired Heads." *Canadian Forum* (December/January).

Rosenfeld, Rachel. 1979. "Women's Occupational Careers: Individual and Structural Explanations." *Sociology of Work and Occupations* 6 (August): 283-311.

Russel, Robert Arnold. 1978. *The Electronic Briefcase: The Office of the Future*. Occasional Paper No. 3. Montreal: The Institute for Research on Public Policy.

Russell, Susan J. 1978. "Sex Role Socialization in High School: A Study in the Perpetuation of Patriarchal Culture." Ph.D. Thesis (Sociology). Toronto: University of Toronto.

Science Council of Canada. 1979. "A Scenario for the Implementation of Interactive Computer-Communications Systems in the Home." A Position Paper of the Science Council Committee on Communications and Computers (T.R. Ide, Chairman). Ottawa: Science Council of Canada.

Science Council of Canada. 1980. *The Impact of Microelectronics Revolution on Work and Working*. "Proceedings of a Workshop sponsored by the Science Council of Canada Committee on Computers and Communications." Ottawa: Minister of Supply and Services Canada.

Seear, B.N. 1971. *Re-entry of Women to the Labor Market After an Interruption of Employment*. Series on Employment of Special Groups, No. 7. Paris: Organisation for Economic Co-operation and Development.

Serafini, S.; Andrieu, M.; and Estabrooks, M. 1978. "Post Industrial Canada and the New Information Technology." *Canadian Futures* 1: 81-91.

Sindell, Peter S. 1979. *Public Policy and the Information Society*. Montreal: GAMMA.

Statistics Canada. 1975. *Canada Year Book 1975*. Cat. No. 11-202. Ottawa: Minister of Industry, Trade and Commerce.

Statistics Canada. 1976. *Labour Force by Level of Schooling—1971 Census of Canada*. Cat. No. 94-786 (advance bulletin). Ottawa: Minister of Industry, Trade and Commerce.

Statistics Canada. 1978*a*. *Historical Labour Force Statistics—Actual Data, Seasonal Factors, Seasonally Adjusted Data, 1953−1966*. Cat. No. 71-201. Ottawa: Minister of Industry, Trade and Commerce.

Statistics Canada. 1978*b*. *Labour Force Activity: Labour Force Participation Rates by Age and Sex and Marital Status and Sex, 1971 and 1976*. Cat. No. 94-804. Ottawa: Minister of Industry, Trade and Commerce.

Statistics Canada. 1978*c*. *1971 Census of Canada*. Vol. 3 (Part 2)—*Labour Force: Occupations, Historical*. Cat. No. 94-716. Ottawa: Minister of Industry, Trade and Commerce.

Statistics Canada. 1979*a*. *Historical Labour Force Statistics—Actual Data, Seasonal Factors, Seasonally Adjusted Data, 1978*. Cat. No. 71-201. Ottawa: Minister of Industry, Trade and Commerce.

Statistics Canada. 1979*b*. *Labour Force Annual Averages: 1975 —1978*. Cat. No. 71-529. Ottawa: Minister of Industry, Trade and Commerce.

Statistics Canada. 1979*c*. *Population Projections for Canada and the Provinces: 1976—2001*. Cat. No. 91-520. Ottawa: Minister of Industry, Trade and Commerce.

Statistics Canada. 1979*d*. *Real Domestic Product by Industry*. Cat. No. 61-213. Ottawa: Minister of Industry, Trade and Commerce.

Statistics Canada. 1980*a*. Unpublished data communicated to the author by the Labour Force Survey Division. Ottawa.

Statistics Canada. 1980*b*. *Employment, Earnings and Hours (December, 1979)*. Cat. No. 72-002. Ottawa: Minister of Industry, Trade and Commerce.

Statistics Canada. 1980*c*. *The Labour Force (December 1979)*. Cat. No. 71-001. Ottawa: Minister of Industry, Trade and Commerce.

Statistics Canada. 1980*d*. *Perspectives Canada III*. Cat. No. 11-511. Ottawa: Minister of Industry, Trade and Commerce.

Statistics Canada. 1980*e*. *Real Domestic Product by Industry*. Cat. No. 61-213. Ottawa: Minister of Industry, Trade and Commerce.

Thompson, Gordon B. 1979. *Memo from Mercury: Information Technology* **Is** *Different*. Occasional Paper No. 10. Montreal: The Institute for Research on Public Policy.

U.S. Bureau of Labor Statistics. 1979. *Technology and Labor in Five Industries* (banking, telephone, retailing, insurance and air transport). Bulletin 2033. Washington, D.C.: U.S. Government Printing Office.

Valaskakis, Kimon. 1979. *The Information Society: The Issues and Choices—Integrating Report, Phase 1*. GAMMA Information Society Project. Montreal: GAMMA.

Weik, Martin H., ed. 1977. *Standard Dictionary of Computers and Information Processing*. Rochelle Park, N.J.: Hayden Book.

Whisler, Thomas L. 1970. *The Impact of Computers on Organizations*. New York: Praeger.

White, Julie. 1980. *Women and Unions*. Ottawa: Canadian Advisory Council on the Status of Women.

WPI (Word Processing International) Ltd. 1977. Unpublished discussion papers prepared for the Office Automation Management Seminar Series. Ottawa.

Working Women. 1980. *Race Against Time: Automation of the Office. An Analysis of Trends in Office Automation and the Impact on the Office Workforce*. Report. Cleveland, Ohio: National Association of Office Workers.

Young, Howard. 1978. *Jobs, Technology, and Hours of Labor: The Future of Work in the U.S.* Paper presented at hearings of the Joint Economic Committee's Special Study on Economic Change, Washington, D.C., 14 June.

Zeman, Z.P. 1979. *The Impacts of Computer/Communications on Employment in Canada: An Overview of Current OECD Debates*. Report prepared for the Department of Communications, Telecommunications Economics Branch. Montreal: The Institute for Research on Public Policy.

Zsigmond, Zoltan. 1979. Unpublished projection produced for the Futures Studies Program, Institute for Research on Public Policy, Montreal. Ottawa: Statistics Canada, Education, Science and Culture Division.

The Institute for Research on Public Policy
PUBLICATIONS AVAILABLE*
March 1982

BOOKS

Leroy O. Stone & Claude Marceau	*Canadian Population Trends and Public Policy Through the 1980s*. 1977 $4.00
Raymond Breton	*The Canadian Condition: A Guide to Research in Public Policy*. 1977 $2.95
Raymond Breton	*Une orientation de la recherche politique dans le contexte canadien*. 1978 $2.95
J.W. Rowley & W.T. Stanbury, eds.	*Competition Policy in Canada: Stage II, Bill C-13*. 1978 $12.95
C.F. Smart & W.T. Stanbury, eds.	*Studies on Crisis Management*. 1978 $9.95
W.T. Stanbury, ed.	*Studies on Regulation in Canada*. 1978 $9.95
Michael Hudson	*Canada in the New Monetary Order: Borrow? Devalue? Restructure!* 1978 $6.95
W.A.W. Neilson & J.C. MacPherson, eds.	*The Legislative Process in Canada: The Need for Reform*. 1978 $12.95
David K. Foot, ed.	*Public Employment and Compensation in Canada: Myths and Realities*. 1978 $10.95
W.E. Cundiff & Mado Reid, eds.	*Issues in Canadian/U.S. Transborder Computer Data Flows*. 1979 $6.50
David K. Foot	*Public Employment in Canada: Statistical Series*. 1979 $15.00
Meyer W. Bucovetsky, ed.	*Studies in Public Employment and Compensation in Canada*. 1979 $14.95
Richard French & André Béliveau	*The RCMP and the Management of National Security*. 1979 $6.95

* Order Address: The Institute for Research on Public Policy
P.O. Box 9300, Station A
TORONTO, Ontario
M5W 2C7

Richard French &
André Béliveau

La GRC et la gestion de la sécurité nationale. 1979
$6.95

Leroy O. Stone &
Michael J. MacLean

*Future Income Prospects for Canada's Senior
Citizens*. 1979 $7.95

Richard Bird (in collaboration
with Bucovetsky & Foot)

The Growth of Public Employment in Canada. 1979
$12.95

G. Bruce Doern &
Allan M. Maslove, eds.

The Public Evaluation of Government Spending.
1979 $10.95

Richard Price, ed.

The Spirit of the Alberta Indian Treaties. 1979
$8.95

Richard J. Schultz

Federalism and the Regulatory Process. 1979
$1.50

Richard J. Schultz

Le fédéralisme et le processus de réglementation.
1979 $1.50

Lionel D. Feldman &
Katherine A. Graham

*Bargaining for Cities. Municipalities and
Intergovernmental Relations: An Assessment*. 1979
$10.95

Elliot J. Feldman &
Neil Nevitte, eds.

*The Future of North America: Canada, the United
States, and Quebec Nationalism*. 1979 $7.95

Maximo Halty-Carrere

*Technological Development Strategies for
Developing Countries*. 1979 $12.95

G.B. Reschenthaler

*Occupational Health and Safety in Canada: The
Economics and Three Case Studies*. 1979 $5.00

David R. Protheroe

*Imports and Politics: Trade Decision-Making in
Canada, 1968–1979*. 1980 $8.95

G. Bruce Doern

*Government Intervention in the Canadian Nuclear
Industry*. 1980 $8.95

G. Bruce Doern &
R.W. Morrison, eds.

Canadian Nuclear Policies. 1980 $14.95

Yoshi Tsurumi with
Rebecca R. Tsurumi

Sogoshosha: Engines of Export-Based Growth.
1980 $8.95

Allan M. Maslove &
Gene Swimmer

*Wage Controls in Canada, 1975–78: A Study of
Public Decision Making*. 1980 $11.95

T. Gregory Kane

Consumers and the Regulators: Intervention in the Federal Regulatory Process. 1980 $10.95

Albert Breton &
Anthony Scott

The Design of Federations. 1980 $6.95

A.R. Bailey &
D.G. Hull

The Way Out: A More Revenue-Dependent Public Sector and How It Might Revitalize the Process of Governing. 1980 $6.95

Réjean Lachapelle &
Jacques Henripin

La situation démolinguistique au Canada : évolution passée et prospective. 1980 $24.95

Raymond Breton,
Jeffrey G. Reitz &
Victor F. Valentine

Cultural Boundaries and the Cohesion of Canada. 1980 $18.95

David R. Harvey

Christmas Turkey or Prairie Vulture? An Economic Analysis of the Crow's Nest Pass Grain Rates. 1980 $10.95

Stuart McFadyen,
Colin Hoskins &
David Gillen

Canadian Broadcasting: Market Structure and Economic Performance. 1980 $15.95

Richard M. Bird

Taxing Corporations. 1980 $6.95

Albert Breton &
Raymond Breton

Why Disunity? An Analysis of Linguistic and Regional Cleavages in Canada. 1980 $6.95

Leroy O. Stone &
Susan Fletcher

A Profile of Canada's Older Population. 1980 $7.95

Peter N. Nemetz, ed.

Resource Policy: International Perspectives. 1980 $18.95

Keith A.J. Hay, ed.

Canadian Perspectives on Economic Relations with Japan. 1980 $18.95

Raymond Breton &
Gail Grant

La langue de travail au Québec : synthèse de la recherche sur la rencontre de deux langues. 1981 $10.95

Diane Vanasse

L'évolution de la population scolaire du Québec. 1981 $12.95

Raymond Breton,
Jeffrey G. Reitz &
Victor F. Valentine

Les frontières culturelles et la cohésion du Canada. 1981 $18.95

H.V. Kroeker, ed.	*Sovereign People or Sovereign Governments.* 1981 $12.95
Peter Aucoin, ed.	*The Politics and Management of Restraint in Government.* 1981 $17.95
David M. Cameron, ed.	*Regionalism and Supranationalism: Challenges and Alternatives to the Nation-State in Canada and Europe.* 1981 $9.95
Heather Menzies	*Women and the Chip.* 1981 $6.95
Nicole S. Morgan	*Nowhere to Go? Possible Consequences of the Demographic Imbalance in Decision-Making Groups of the Federal Public Service.* 1981 $8.95
Nicole S. Morgan	*Où aller? Les conséquences prévisibles des déséquilibres démographiques chez les groupes de décision de la fonction publique fédérale.* 1981 $8.95
Peter N. Nemetz, ed.	*Energy Crisis: Policy Response.* 1981 $10.95
Allan Tupper & G. Bruce Doern, eds.	*Public Corporations and Public Policy in Canada.* 1981 $16.95
James Gillies	*Where Business Fails.* 1981 $9.95
Réjean Lachapelle & Jacques Henripin	*The Demolinguistic Situation in Canada: Past Trends and Future Prospects.* 1981 $24.95

OCCASIONAL PAPERS

W.E. Cundiff (No. 1)	*Nodule Shock? Seabed Mining and the Future of the Canadian Nickel Industry.* 1978 $3.00
IRPP/Brookings (No. 2)	*Conference on Canadian-U.S. Economic Relations.* 1978 $3.00
Robert A. Russel (No. 3)	*The Electronic Briefcase: The Office of the Future.* 1978 $3.00
C.C. Gotlieb (No. 4)	*Computers in the Home: What They Can Do for Us—And to Us.* 1978 $3.00
Raymond Breton & Gail Grant Akian (No. 5)	*Urban Institutions and People of Indian Ancestry.* 1978 $3.00

K.A. Hay
(No. 6)

Friends or Acquaintances? Canada and Japan's Other Trading Partners in the Early 1980s.
1979 $3.00

T. Atkinson
(No. 7)

Trends in Life Satisfaction Among Canadians, 1968 – 1977. 1979 $3.00

Fred Thompson &
W.T. Stanbury
(No. 9)

The Political Economy of Interest Groups in the Legislative Process in Canada. 1979 $3.00

Pierre Sormany
(No. 11)

Les micro-esclaves : vers une bio-industrie canadienne. 1979 $3.00

Zavis P. Zeman &
David Hoffman, eds.
(No. 13)

The Dynamics of the Technological Leadership of the World. 1980 $3.00

Russell Wilkins
(No. 13*a*)

Health Status in Canada, 1926 – 1976.
1980 $3.00

Russell Wilkins
(No. 13*b*)

L'état de santé au Canada, 1926 – 1976.
1980 $3.00

P. Pergler
(No. 14)

The Automated Citizen: Social and Political Impact of Interactive Broadcasting. 1980 $4.95

Donald G. Cartwright
(No. 16)

Official Language Populations in Canada: Patterns and Contacts. 1980 $4.95

REPORT
Dhiru Patel

Dealing With Interracial Conflict: Policy Alternatives. 1980 $5.95

Robert A. Russel

Office Automation: Key to the Information Society.
1981 $3.00

Irving Brecher

Canada's Competition Policy Revisited: Some New Thoughts on an Old Story. 1982 $3.00